Personal Branding Strategies:

The Ultimate Practical Guide To Branding And Marketing Yourself Online Through Instagram, YouTube, Facebook And Twitter And How To Utilize Advertising On Social Media

By Gary Clyne

Table of Contents

Section One:

"Social media changes the relationship between companies and customers from master and servant, to peer-to-peer."

-Jay Baer

Introduction:

There is a rising new class of online influencers who are turning social media into a lucrative platform for selling brands. Would you like to make lots of cash, enjoy a glamorous lifestyle and travel the world as well? Then you've come to the right place!

Scroll through some of these highly paid social media influencers, and you'll see how glamorous their lives seem to be. Posting stunning photos and showing off some of the best locations in the world to their thousands or at times millions of followers. It's no wonder many people want to become online influencers.

If you've spent some time on YouTube, Instagram or Facebook I'm sure you've seen how some individuals appear to be living a dreamy vacation lifestyle. Taking pictures in exotic beaches like Bora Bora, Bali and Maldives, posing like fashionistas in front of the Arch de Triomphe in Paris or enjoying winter in a beautiful cabin somewhere on the French Alps.

Most social media influencers tend to include on their captions information about their outfits, accessories, and the prestigious locations they are visiting along with a long list of hashtags. And then almost indistinguishable from all the other images on their feed, you'll usually find a hashtag #ad at the end of the captions.

With that slight difference on the post, you get a glimpse on how influencers are monetizing their influence on Instagram or any other social platform. And by monetization, I'm talking as high as six-figure income earners on Instagram. Some Instagrammers can demand $20,000 for a single post, and the crazy thing is, companies are more than willing to pay these hefty fees.

As it turns out, being an influencer isn't a constant vacation. For many of these social media influencers, it's a full-time job. These men and women consider themselves to be social media influencers and marketing professionals who are helping transform traditional marketing and advertising.

Now I know what you might be thinking. How in the world do I get to 88,000 followers on social media when I've barely begun?

Well, it's good to mention here that most of the social media rockstars your see, whether they are Instagrammers or YouTubers started working on their accounts while in high school. It often begins as a hobby posting images around fashion, beauty, video games and other products.

And they are involved in this for years before they ever become highly paid influencers with hundreds of thousands of followers. But you don't need to have such a massive following to monetize your online influence, and it doesn't even matter if you're just starting out.

If you get thrilled anytime you think of yourself as a social media influencer sharing your passion with the world, then you're definitely the right fit for this book. You'll learn how to build your personal brand and a captivated audience, so that big brands can start paying you to post online.

In our digitally connected world where more time is spent online interacting with various types of content and engaging in conversations, savvy individuals are spotting an opportunity of a lifetime. Have you?

Chances are you've acquired this book because you're already aware of the emerging opportunity to design a lifestyle business that richly rewards you and enables you to do more of the things you love.

A few years ago I started noticing a significant shift on platforms like YouTube and Facebook. Everyday people were building large communities, creating content and attracting significant opportunities from well-known brands, which turned into lucrative deals. When Instagram came along, I didn't pay much attention to it. As a regular blogger (though it was still a hobby at the time), I made the mistake of underestimating the significant trend that Instagram would start, and although it took me a while, I quickly caught on.

I have watched as me, and my friends go from zero followers on Instagram to making $15,000 a month within the first year of growing our lifestyle brands and although I'm not here to make any claims, I am confident that the strategies I'm about to share with you could very well take you from an unknown person to a social media influencer in a matter of months.

Of course, that actual result is entirely dependent on your commitment, efforts, and ability to implement these proven strategies.

What started out as a hobby for me has turned out to be a life-changing experience, and I hope that as you go through this book, you too, will begin to see the unexplored potential in your life that's just waiting to be unleashed into the world.

When it comes to owning your life, creating your own economy and living life on your own terms, no path could be better and more enjoyable than that of building a personal brand and becoming a social media influencer.

Big brand and fortune 500 companies are desperate to pour some of their marketing budgets on influencers who have done the work and built out responsive, highly engaged tribes. And I know for a fact that your interest, curiosity or desire to become as successful as some of the people you've seen either while swiping through Instagram or binge-watching on YouTube is the main reason you picked up this book. So I don't want to waste any more time, let's cut to the chase and help you learn the ropes that will get you a lucrative online brand.

Before you can figure out "the how" it's always prudent to understand "the what." So let's start with the what.

This book is divided into sections to make your learning experience practical and easy to navigate. After perusing so many books on this topic, I realized most of them were totally confusing and overwhelming. I don't want you to feel confused or overwhelmed. That's why every section is jam-packed with simple, easy to follow strategies.

I do however recommend you go through it in the order presented if you wish to get the most out of it. In section one as I said, we focus on the fundamentals. Understanding what you're getting into when you decide to become an influencer.

In section two we talk about the strategies, planning and how to build your community of delighted and engaged followers. We also talk about the power of creating world-class content and why you need to prioritize that.

In section three we talk about packaging and marketing your brand, as well as the difference between marketing and advertising that so many people trip over. I also share some valuable tips and guidelines to help you stay on the right side of the law especially as your business starts growing.

In section four we do a deep dive into the various platforms that you can establish yourself as an influencer as well as how to set them up the right way. I literally break down each of the leading platforms, I tell you how each of them works and how to make them work for you.

By the time we get to the last chapter of this section, the only thing you'll need is the step-by-step framework you can deploy immediately (which I provide in chapter nine) so that you can build your brand and become an influencer within the next few months.

But wait; let's not get ahead of ourselves here. We need to warm up the engine first in preparation for takeoff. And the best way to accomplish that is by answering two simple questions: What is a personal brand and why do you need a personal brand if you want to become a social media influencer?

What Is Personal Branding?

My mom likes to tell a story from my childhood about my obsession with soda. So embarrassing, but I'll still share it with you anyway. When I was a toddler, and we were taking a trip to the store or a friend's house, they would put me in the backseat of our Toyota in a child's car seat. As we drove down the highway, I would see ads or signposts with a lot of red and a bottle of some kind, and I would yell, "Cola!"

Now, I was only about three years old at the time, so I could barely read, but I had learned to pronounce the word "soda" and "Cola." Each time something reminded me of the red patterns on the Coke bottle, I would yell out loud in excitement hoping my mom would let me have some. I learned at a very young age to associate Coca-Cola and the taste of soda (as well as the sugar rush which I obviously loved) with the color red.

That is the power of branding.

Nike, Airbnb, Coca Cola, Ferrari, Amazon, and Apple. These are just a few business brand names that are recognized worldwide. You undoubtedly know these brands and understand the concept of a business brand.

Chances are, you're also familiar with names such as Beyoncé, The Kardashians, Tiger Woods, Richard Branson, and Oprah, just to name a few. Whatever your biases and personal opinions might be of these individuals, there's no denying you've heard of some or all of these names. They are a classic example of what we call a personal brand.

In our new digital age and the emergence of smartphones and social media, the typical personal brand has gotten a makeover. Personal branding was usually associated with celebrities and the rich and famous. Not anymore.

Things are shifting, personal branding is evolving and thanks to the power of peer-to-peer engagement through mobile devices, personal branding has expanded to include more than just blue-collar children and multimillion-dollar businesses or celebrities.

I am sure you've already been sensing this shift. Even if at first it may seem unusual to most people, the concept of personal branding especially when it comes to social media and influencer marketing requires a dynamic definition. That's why before establishing yourself as an influencer I recommend polishing your personal brand.

The simplest definition of a personal brand that I can give you is this:

Your personal brand is the combination of your skills, experiences, achievements, actions, personality and all the content you share within a given community, industry or the marketplace both online and offline. It's the representation of who you are and the impression others perceive.

In today's world, people start by Googling your name to figure out who you are. They make an assumption of you based on what they find online whether the information is accurate or not.

It makes sense then, to polish up and deliberately work on building a personal brand that is congruent with how you want the world to perceive you as well as the products you sell. Personal branding, therefore, becomes the consistent and intentional process of creating an important public perception, so that you can be viewed as an authority and someone who is credible enough to be trusted.

Why Build A Personal Brand?

Perception is everything in today's world. Deliberately building a personal brand as you grow your influencer business gives you the opportunity to make sure others perceive you in the most beneficial way. It gives you control over your self-image as well as your overall brand and enables you to highlight your strengths and passions.

The more authentic you can be across the board, the easier it will be for people to trust you and as we all know, influencer marketing is ultimately about building a community that believes in you. When people feel like they know, like and trust you (even if they never met you in person), they are more likely to buy whatever you have to offer.

If you want to become influential, you need a strong personal brand. There's just no shortcutting this part of your business growth.

And the best part about working on your personal brand is that it helps you stand out from the crowd. No one else can be you, so when you learn how to integrate that uniqueness into your business strategically, you become one-of-a-kind and memorable.

As millennials continue to gain more spending power, their distrust of traditional marketing and advertising continues to grow. Research has shown that 84% of millennials have a hard time trusting both big brands and the dry advertisements they create. But this same group is prepared to believe people they feel like they "know."

As a result of this shift in consumer behavior, businesses have to rethink how they market and advertise. In fact, the main reason influencer marketing has become so huge in the last couple of years is due to this movement towards connection with a real person in a business rather than an impersonal brand.

Of course, when the business is small, it's easier to make the shift. For bigger companies, however, it has become a significant challenge that they are hoping to overcome by the use of influencer marketing. I assume that's the gap you intend to fill with your business as a social media influencer? If yes, then take the time to self-reflect, introspect and thoughtfully design your personal brand from a foundation of knowing yourself.

Your personal brand needs to match your values, mission, and purpose as well as your targeted clientele. It's about consciously building up your reputation in a way that aligns with the area of expertise you wish to become known for.

Think for a moment of a well-known figure in the adult entertainment industry - Hugh Hefner.

Hefner had a personal brand long before the term even existed, and he's lived out his entire life portraying the lifestyle a true playboy would have. He gave his readers a matching image to what he was selling thus enhancing his Playboy empire in a very congruent way. His readers have continued to be loyal to the brand because he represents it accordingly.

You want your brand and everything else you do to be just as congruent and relatable to your potential and existing clients. The more you do this, the faster your influence will grow.

Chapter 02: Influencer Marketing

Influencer marketing is the name we've given to a hybrid process that integrates old and new marketing tools and techniques. It takes the idea of the celebrity endorsement and places it into a modern-day content-driven marketing campaign.

The main difference, however, is that influencer marketing is about developing genuine relationships. Unlike celebrity endorsements, which were usually superficial and purely transactional arrangements, influencer marketing helps both the brand and the influencer. As the influencer helps create greater visibility for a brand's product or service, the influencer better serves his or her audience, grows a new enriching relationship with the brand being promoted and the brand, in turn, increases its reach and potential sales.

As more people continue to use the Internet, shopping online is becoming a standard way of life. The impact of traditional media is continuing to wear off because, at the end of the day, it's about getting consumer attention. And in today's market, attention is online, especially on social platforms. This, in short, is the reason behind the growing industry commonly referred to as influencer marketing. Simply stated, those with large, engaged audiences now possess more power than most traditional media.

As more prominent brands recognize this trend, they are choosing to invest their marketing and advertising dollars on said individuals and truth be told, it is a wise investment because consumers today are more interested in personalization.

According to Wikipedia, Influencer marketing also known as influence marketing is a form of marketing in which focus is placed on influential people rather than the target market as a whole on social media. In other words, it's about identifying savvy individuals who have influence over a specific group on potential customers online and crafting marketing activities around these influences.

Influencer marketing derives its value from three core sources:

Original content: This is where you as an influencer create unique, engaging content. The content needs to be useful, purposeful and it needs to be a mix of information that grows your brand as well as the brands you choose to promote.

Consumer trust: This is where you build and maintain strong relationships with your carefully cultivated audience. Your audience is the key to your success. It's your job to win the trust of your audience (tribe as I like to call it) because the more they trust and feel connected to you, the more they will value your opinion and anything you have to sell.

Social reach: This is your ability to reach millions of consumers through your social channels and blogging platform.

What makes an influencer

To give a firm and rigid answer to this question is to limit a very dynamic industry. No one-liner can fully identify what an influencer is or what makes one. There are always varying factors that lead to one becoming an influencer, and if you ask 10 different experts what it takes to become an influencer, you'll come out with 10 different answers. One thing is certain, however. Influencer marketing depends mainly on the context and the medium of influence communication whether that is online, offline or both.

An influencer can be a buyer, or he or she may be a third party existing either in the supply chain as a retailer, manufacturer, etc. Or they could be value-adding influencers such as academics, industry analysts, journalists, and professional advisers.

As a paid influencer you receive a product, service or experience, either for free or heavily discounted with the final goal that you will use your networking skills and social media following to spread good vibes about that particular product or service with the ultimate aim of generating more business for the brand.

Can anyone become an influencer?

Due to the fact that influencer marketing revolves around ordinary everyday people with a captivated audience, I am convinced that anyone anywhere can become a social media influencer. But perhaps not everyone should. It takes a certain level of commitment, planning, and persistence to really succeed in this industry. One must develop a thick skin and come from a mindset of abundance and collaboration; otherwise, things could get really ugly.

More importantly, you really need to be passionate about becoming an influencer and have a drive that enables you to keep going even when things get tough and trust me, they will!

The journey ahead is full of obstacles and naysayers. Getting people to follow and believe in your ideas doesn't come easy, so you need to be sure this is what you want to do with your life at least for the next couple of years. If it does feel like the path you need to be on, then help make the journey a bit more pleasant by avoiding these rookie mistakes that many newbies get caught up in.

Mistakes to avoid if you want to succeed as a social media influencer

As with any business, if you want to succeed as a social media influencer, there are certain pitfalls you're better off avoiding as you construct your campaigns and grow your brand. The more aware you are of certain blind spots that usually destroy success in this industry, the better equipped you will be as you grow and scale your business. Here are a few.

Mistake #1: Buying your followers

This has to be one of the worst mistakes an aspiring social media influencer could make. And yet so many still do. First of all, you should know that social platforms would punish you greatly if you buy followers.

For example, Greg Jones experienced firsthand how unforgiving Instagram is when he made this grievous mistake of giving his account a little boost. He felt he wasn't growing fast enough. After a year of daily posting and engagement, he only had a little over 5,000 followers. He figured it would take too long to get to 100,000 (which was his goal). And so he bought some followers and overnight went from under 10,000 to over 100,000 followers. Soon after that, his account was forcibly shut down. Ouch!

If you are serious about being an influencer, play the long game and don't let anyone convince you that any good can possibly come from buying followers. Avoid this mistake like the plague itself!

Mistake #2: Focusing only on follower counts

Oftentimes big brands and companies will target a social media influencer based on their follower count. The larger the number, the easier it becomes to get paid... Or so it used to be!

It's easy to conclude that the more followers you have, the better, but this isn't the case anymore. I'm not saying follower count doesn't matter, but it's not the only factor to take into account nowadays. Recently, all social media platforms including Instagram have upgraded their systems providing us with the capability to measure more metrics, and companies are becoming aware that followership doesn't equal engagement or responsiveness.

In the chapter on platforms, you'll learn how to set up your account the right way on these social platforms so you can have access to the necessary insights and metrics.

If your audience is unresponsive to your content, it doesn't matter how large the number is, you won't be in a position to charge high fees or get the job done well for your clients. Don't overlook the power of engagement as you build your tribe. Sometimes a smaller following can be just as lucrative for you and the brands you work with.

Mistake #3: Staring with no proper planning

You must have a precise and detailed plan if you want to succeed in this industry. Strategy at every phase is essential. You need to have a business plan, a branding document, a documented content strategy plan, a content plan, and editorial calendar, a content inventory strategy and you also need a framework that helps you serve brands that want to hire you.

Clarity is everything when starting out and it will ensure you build a solid business so don't skip over the planning and strategizing phase of your business development.

Mistake #4: Getting into it for the money

This is a common one especially for so-called "fitness influencers." They hear the money is good and get excited about the thought of becoming an online celebrity so rather than building a client-focused business, they focus on what's in it for them.

This is the best way to dip yourself into imminent failure. Whatever recognition or social fame you manage to gather will be very fleeting if you're just "using" your community to make money and become famous. There's no easy way to say this to you, but if money is your biggest priority, find other ways of acquiring it that doesn't involve taking advantage of this human need for "love and belonging" which is what a community is meant to be.

Mistake #5: Relying on Bots

If patience, persistence, and hard work don't come naturally to you, this industry will probably not yield much profit long term. Influencer marketing is always about playing the long game.

Equally as bad as buying followers is using bots to grow your community. Relying on bots to do the work for you essentially makes you a cheater. Bots can never substitute the real and raw human interaction necessary to build a true community.

Growing a strong follower count that positions you as an expert and influencer is laborious but that is indeed the only way you'll be able to monetize your role as an influencer.

Mistake #6: Replying to comments slowly or not at all

As I said before, there is great power in engagement within your tribe. The more people share, comment and interact with your content the higher you rank on Google as well as in the eyes of brands that are looking for influencers in your space.

You can only get people to interact by demonstrating that you care about each and every individual on your list, especially in the beginning. You must reply promptly to the comments people leave you even if it's a simple thank you for a simple compliment. Encourage conversations by asking your followers a question in your captions or posts.

Respond even when it's uncomfortable for you or if someone doesn't react the way you'd hoped. Remember all feedback is valuable. These small actions on your end go a long way to show your followers that you genuinely care about them and their opinions.

Now that you know which pitfalls to avoid, you're on the right path to setting up and growing a community and business that will attract big brand opportunities. Before jumping into the strategy sections, let's make sure we have clarity on the business you wish to have.

Start with the end in mind

If you enjoy spending time on social media platforms and feel passionate about a particular topic or niche, then you'll definitely enjoy the perks of being an influence. However, this business still requires the same structure and planning as would any other. And the best place to begin is always with the end in mind as Stephen Covey taught in his book.

The fact that you will spend most of your time interacting with people, trying to influence their behavior, thoughts, opinions and even purchase decisions means you need to know what motivates you. You can only show up as your best version to serve a growing audience when you understand your motivations, objectives and who you are.

Invest some time at this phase of your business to paint a clear vision of what you ultimately want to experience as an influencer. You need to understand your core values, the priorities that matter to you, the purpose behind your business and the mission you will serve. The more clarity you have on this end picture, the easier it becomes to design a lifestyle and business you'll love.

Practical exercise:

Here are some questions to self-reflect upon. Take a journal or notebook and answer each one with as much detail as you can before moving on to section two.

1. What are my core values?

2. What is my life vision?

3. What am I passionate about or very interested in?

4. What are my superpowers (the things I do better than everyone I know)?

5. What are 5 words that describe me?

6. What is my story?

7. What most strongly sets me apart from my peers?

8. What issue/problem am I trying to solve?

9. Why does resolving this problem matter to me?

10. What is my most prominent belief about myself?

11. What are my strengths, weaknesses and current opportunities that I need to become aware of?

12. How do I represent myself?

13. Are there any changes/improvements I want to make?

14. Why am I choosing to become an influencer?

15. Why does becoming a highly paid influencer matter to me?

16. How will becoming a highly paid influencer change my life?

17. Where do I see my business going?

18. What is the biggest challenge I'm facing now?

19. What are my short-term business goals?

20. What are my long-term business goals?

21. What is the fundamental purpose behind my brand and this business I am building?

22. What mission do I want to serve through my brand?

23. What is the value I promise to deliver to my audience?

24. What is the value I promise to provide to my paying clients?

25. What are my deal breakers when it comes to accepting paid brand contracts?

26. Why should the market believe in my ideas and me?

27. Do I feel like I am the right and credible person to take on this role?

Key highlights from this section:

• Personal branding is a must for anyone who wants to become an influencer in any industry. As such you must diligently work on developing a strong personal brand online.

• Big brands and fortune 500 companies are very eager to invest in influencer marketing because they anticipate a good return on investment. In other words, they are out there looking to partner with you right now.

• Anyone can become a social media influencer today and build a large community of active members.

• To become a social media influencer requires very little capital but it does need someone with the right work ethics, a strong, abundant mindset and the heart to serve others.

• You must play the long game and think long-term if you want to become wealthy, successful and influential in your space.

• Like any business, there must be a precise strategic plan of implementation if you want this business to succeed.

• The road to success is filled with many pitfalls, many of which can be avoided with a little awareness and a real grasp of who you are and how you want to run your business.

• Getting to know who you are, what your values are, what your purpose is and the mission you will serve is a critical component of ensuring your business is established on the right foundation. So be sure to complete the practical exercise on self-reflection and self-inventory.

Section Two:

"People want to do business with you because you help them get what they want. They don't do business with you to help you get what you want."

- Don Crowther

Chapter 03: Building your Tribe

Whether you realize this or not, becoming an influencer has very little to do with you and everything to do with the audience you build. People are your biggest asset. And if you're not excited about learning everything you can about the people you want to connect with, there's little hope for success in your horizon.

The business of social media influence is centered around an actively engaged community. I like to call it a tribe.

This is because when you approach your efforts in growing an audience with this nurturing mindset, you tend to make all the right moves. A tribe is more than just an audience gathering together on your page. These are your people. They resonate with your perspective and worldview, and they feel a special bond, which is all-important when it comes to selling anything.

Therefore rather than building an audience, I encourage you to focus on building a tribe of people who are passionate about what you do and can't wait to hear from you. At the end of the day, the power lies with this tribe. You can only become a superstar influencer if your tribe decides you are one and it's your job to help influence that outcome.

One of the key ideas I'd like to share with you is that your tribe doesn't just exist online. Yes, they will spend a lot of time on the social platform, but these are real people going to work, going to the gym, shopping in supermarkets and eating in restaurants. Therefore, as you build your influence, get creative. Find ways to nurture your tribe both online and offline. It may just fast track your business growth.

How to get your ideal audience to notice and fall in love with you

It's easy to get someone to fall in love with you when they feel attracted to you. It's also easy to get someone to fall in love with you when they feel seen and understood by you. Your job as an influencer is to be a valuable go-to person for your audience. You need to be that virtual friend that makes them feel like they matter and that they belong. And it begins with the content you post.

Brands want to work with an influencer who is persuasive. Someone who receives positive responses and initiates ongoing conversations within his/her tribe.

There are many ways to go about establishing such a relationship with your tribe. Start with these few and keep upgrading as you grow.

Share your story and help your tribe connect it to their own

Storytelling is the new power play in marketing and advertising. The brands that do it well shall continue to win even during the worst of times. If you learn to integrate storytelling in your business, you will stand out authentically and win.

Storytelling really helps you connect with your audience. My recommendation is that you create a story brand script that allows your tribe to connect your story with their own journey.

Consider all the great movies that you've ever watched and loved. The thing that hooked you and made it so memorable was the fact that you could relate. You experienced the character's story as your own. That's what you want to help your tribe experience as much as possible.

Human beings in today's digitally connected world have an attention span that is shorter than a goldfish according to expert reports. And retaining mundane data or information is always hard for an average person so if you want to stand out use storytelling to connect your brand, and the products you represent to your growing tribe.

Get Creative

Social media platforms are crowded, and there are a lot of influencers trying to capture the attention of your audience. You need to be original as well as highly creative. Figure out ways to get creative so you can get more attention.

Try different features on your chosen platforms as well. Now that most platforms offer several features incorporate all of them as much as you can to see which one gets your followers more fired up and excited.

Lead with your passion

Connect your tribe with your ideas, desires and the mission you serve. If you are an activist for something or an expert educator in a particular field, share this information with your growing tribe. Help them understand your "WHY" and if you do a good job tying it in with their interests, it will create a strong bond.

A community is built and sustained not by logos and fancy graphics but by shared beliefs and ideas.

Create, quality, engaging content consistently

Although we are going to dive deeper into the importance of content creation in chapter four, this is one of the critical aspects of growing your tribe that must be mentioned here. Your content will become the introduction your audience experiences so you must do your research right. Figure out which types of content work best across each platform for the tribe you wish to nurture. Make sure it's high-quality content. The more people believe in your content, the higher your chances of growing an influential brand.

Publish this content consistently, diligently do your research and make sure you produce killer content that can be repurposed across many channels. Then allow yourself to be adaptable across each platform.

Stay relevant and true to your topic

In today's digital landscape, it doesn't matter how many times a day you post as long as what you post is relevant and engaging. If you're the type of influencer who continuously posts unrelated, self-promotional products people will consider you spammy, and you'll lose.

As much as it does help to publish lots of content regularly in this line of work, quality matters more, and it's important you realize that social media content needs to have an intended audience, purpose, and goal.

Your social feed shouldn't be cluttered and filled with spammy information. It needs to have a clear message that appeals to a specific niche. Your aesthetics, framing and messaging needs to be true to you and in resonance with the audience receiving it. The more you hit that sweet spot, the more your audience will engage and continue to follow you.

Finding a sustainable interest or passion

Do you know why most social media influencers start out strong only to hit a brick wall? Or why so many still make little to nothing for their hard efforts even though Forbes reports that an influencer with 100,000 followers can easily earn around $5,000 for a single post?

The main reason is that influencers skip over the critical step of finding a niche that suits their interest. In the next few minutes, I'm going to be helping you narrow down your focus, figure out your topic or niche and establish your authentic voice. But before we do, here's a simple example of what you must never do.

Stephanie Shukle is aspiring to become a social media influencer. When we first met for our consultation session, I quickly realized she had chosen a niche (weight loss for brides) not because she was passionate or even interested in brides but because she'd heard there was lots of money to be made.

This is the fast route to never making it as an influencer. It wasn't sustainable; she wouldn't enjoy consistently creating high-quality original content, or investing countless hours and late nights working on getting the attention of brides hanging out online. Yet she was willing to do it for the money. After taking her through the series of self-reflective questions I gave you in section one (I assume you answered every question too), it was clear this wouldn't be a self-sustaining interest.

The critical takeaway lesson here is to find the alignment between your chosen niche and what you're passionate or at least interested in. You'll devote a lot of time; sweat equity, resources and money into growing this business so it might as well be something you're interested in. To be a successful influencer long term, make sure you choose the niche that most interests you, which also has a large enough audience that consumer brands will be interested in targeting.

Establishing clarity in your voice and finding your niche

Choosing your niche and developing a clear voice go hand in hand. I know they can seem daunting and tough to navigate when you're building your brand, but I will try to simplify the process as much as possible.

After all, the last thing you want is to build a brand that you can't stand!

Although it's easy to look at people like Tony Robbins and Gary Vee and think they became who they are through mere strategy, the truth is, they have evolved over time. You just need to look at their first videos to see what I mean. Their "voice" has matured and changed over time to match the demands of their audience, and in turn, they've become very profitable.

I think it's pointless to stress too much over finding your place and your voice in your space.

You start where you are with what you've got. Do the best you can to be true to yourself and keep evolving as you grow with the business.

All you need to do especially, in the beginning, is just speak about your subject matter in an intelligent and inspiring way. As a natural consequence, your voice will unfold. Test things out as much as you can and learn from the feedback you receive. At the end of the day, your audience and the marketplace are what shape the way you talk about your topic (your voice) and the more you stay open to hearing what people truly want from you, the easier it will be to refine how you get your message across to produce the outcome you most desire.

When it comes to finding your space and picking your niche, specialization is key. So make sure you do some due diligence and answer the following questions before taking that leap of faith.

Practical exercise:

Pick up your journal once again and let's do a little actual training.

1. What are you passionate about?
Get more detailed here. If you're not sure about your passions, then write down the things you find interesting enough. When you don't like dealing with the subject matter or the people in your industry for extended hours daily, you won't have the drive needed to push through tough times as you rise to success.

2. Are there other buyers interested in my niche?

This is where research begins. It's essential to research on your topic because you want to make sure there's a market for your niche and that people are spending money.

If you pick something that's too small or where buyers don't exist it's going to be tough getting brands to work with you because they won't see the ROI of the partnership. Using Google Trends, Facebook, Instagram and other social platforms you can be able to determine whether your chosen niche works.

3. Are there other influencers in my niche?

Contrary to what you might have heard growing up, competition is a good thing. You want to know that there is someone in your space doing something similar to what you want to do and they are crushing it already. And when you seek out influencers, aim for people who are already where you desire to be.

4. How will I monetize my niche?

While I have gone deeper into the monetization of your influencer business in another book, let me share a few insights here. Carve out a clear path to the money in the niche you've chosen. Make sure there are both buyers and sellers of products and services that appeal to you. Do some due diligence on the brands that are active in your niche and figure out the channels and methodologies these brands are using to communicate with their customers.

The more clarity you gain as you answer these questions, the clearer your voice will be. Sharing a consistent message across all your platforms will be easy.

Choosing your message

It's time to bring out your whiteboard and sticky notes. Everything about this next phase will be work in progress, but you must start from somewhere. Never assume that once you define your message, everything else is done.

In your line of work, everything depends on the feedback you get from the audience, which means it will be a constant process of reiteration from the first message you decide to use. Once you put yourself out there and start sharing your message, get feedback and data to see how the clients respond, and then make the necessary adjustments to your brand's messaging.

Practical exercise:

1. Start by defining what makes your brand unique or different.

It needs to be something valuable to your customers, and it must articulate aspects of your business that cost you something to uphold.

Come up with 5 -10 key differentiators and write some supporting details for the ones that stick out. Then finally chose one of these to use as your main statement of reference for now.

2. Develop your one-liner

Also called a tagline. It should capture the essence of what you and your brand represents and how you serve your customer. Take into account your core values, mission statement and the differentiation statement you just created in section one. Write down 10-20 one-liners at a minimum. You may find that you end up going down a creative path with one particular idea or word so cluster those ones into the same group.

In the end, you might have 4 or more clusters with many one-liners. Just let these ideas flow without judgment. There is no right or wrong. In the end, you will find one that stands out and meets all the criterion often associated with awesome taglines.

An example of this would be from Apple: Think Different. Ideally, your one-liner should be memorable, intriguing, and unique to your brand and personality and it shouldn't be more than a sentence. If you can't decide on the perfect fit, survey your friends or even your growing audience and let them participate as you grow your brand.

3. Create your elevator pitch

As much as people think being a social media influencer is about taking selfies and messing around lazily on social feeds throughout the day, this is a real business that requires real strategy and frameworks.

Moreover, to become a highly paid influencer requires you to connect with brands that are willing and looking to work with an influencer. When that opportunity presents itself, you need to be ready and equipped. That's where your elevator pitch comes in.

You need to have a strong elevator pitch so that you can easily communicate your brand to those who don't know you in the shortest time frame possible without losing their attention. The reason it's called an elevator pitch is that it should essentially be communicated in the brief amount of time it takes to go up a few floors in an elevator.

When giving your elevator pitch to strangers and potential brands that you want to work with, make sure you inspire the person enough desire more information. Explain what you do in a tone that gives the person an idea of what it's like to work with you or be in your world.

Below I share the key things your elevator pitch needs to have to generate a reaction that will please you.

• Start with your "who."

Get to know who makes up your audience. Do you have moms? Dads? Teens? Vegans?

The more you know about your audience, the easier it will be to identify a potential brand that would be interested in working with you. Check your Google Analytics and Social Media insights to know more about your audience and their behavioral patterns. You can learn the age range, gender and location from all the major social platforms when you have a business account. But don't stop there. You need to know the psychographics of your audience as well.

Let's assume your audience is dads. What are their hobbies? What other influencers or magazines or books do they follow? Where do they mostly like to hang out online?

Of course, getting such details is tougher if you're just relying on analytics so strategically engage and interact more with your audience. The more time you spend directly conversing with your audience, the better you'll know them.

One of the best ways to do this live interaction is through live video streams. Aside from the fact that Facebook, Instagram, and LinkedIn are pushing out video content above all others (which means you'll get more reach), people enjoy consuming video content. Through Facebook Live, Instagram Live or Instagram

Stories, your audience will get the opportunity to decide if they genuinely like you and your brand. It also gives you the chance to know more about them.

If you also have a list already built, that's another excellent way to discover more about your audience. Share more of your personal stories and relate them back to your mission and brand. Ask questions and encourage direct responses so that your audience can feel comfortable enough sharing their stories as well. Regardless of the channels you use, make sure you prioritize knowing as much as you can about your audience before going to pitch potential brands.

• Figure out the pain point and the solution:

Once you know your audience, it's time to hone your message. More specifically - what solution do you have for the brands you want to work with?

Your audience has a pain point or problem that they feel you help solve or remedy. Do you have clarity on what that is? It could be something as simple as knowing which baby bottle brand to get for their newborn or which perfume to buy for Valentines. It could be what types of clothes a man should wear to improve their personal appearance and increase self-confidence.

Whatever your audience routinely comes to you for, will become an opportunity for you to collaborate with brands because when a brand realizes that you can influence people to purchase a particular product, they will be very eager to work with you.

Again, going back to analytics and using data to inform us on our pitch, we can be able to track the content that performs the best. At times we might think our audience comes to us for one thing only to discover they care more about a topic we didn't even think was relevant. For example, if you're an influencer sharing content around healthy vegetarian food, you might think people come to you for healthy tips, but when you go through the backend data, you realize they actually come to you for comforting vegetarian recipes. By gaining this realization, you're better equipped to identify the problem that you actually solve, and it empowers you to attract more of your ideal audience as well as relevant brands.

• Test to make sure the elevator pitch makes sense and answers the right question satisfactorily:

For this to work, you'll need some practice. Pause for a moment and imagine you're standing in an elevator with the CEO of a cool brand you'd love to work with.

He asks you, what is it you do?

What would be your answer to that? You want to make sure the elevator pitch you create is a perfect statement answering that question. As you craft, your elevator pitch think from the question, incorporate the various aspects I've outlined in this entire chapter and make sure you compress it into something short, concise and straightforward enough for this CEO to get before he jumps off the elevator.

If you can do this right, you'll not only create a killer elevator pitch, but you'll also gain real followers fast!

4. Have a stunning bio and "about me" page

The more people can clearly understand who you are and what you do, the easier it will be to attract the right audience and the right brands. That means you need to have your bio in all relevant places online. Even if you don't have a website, you can use sites like Wix and About Me.com to set up a professional bio that dives deep into who you are and what you do.

Crafting your message

If your message doesn't resonate with your audience, it becomes really tough to grow as an influencer and attract high paying brands. In today's noisy world, finding your message and making sure your audience shares the same view is critical.

Don't be confused by this idea of honing down your messaging. At this point I am not referring to your brand identity (that can come later), I am focusing purely on what matters to your audience. You can only find your message when you understand what your audience truly cares about and then tie it in with your brand's mission and values.

There's massive competition in the world of social media influencing. It's not enough to hang your hat and post a few selfies every day. You need to actually stand out from the crowd and become recognized for a particular topic. Maximize Social Business suggests that there are around eight million active "mommy bloggers" in the world. Can you imagine how competitive that area must be if you want to stand out?

You'd need to have a pretty loud voice to heard. But then again, being the loudest online doesn't necessarily mean you'll do well. People might just tag you as noisy or spammy especially if you're also promoting brands and products.

Regardless of your chosen niche, if it's a thriving market, there's bound to be plenty of competition. So rather than trying to be a loud mouth why not focus all your energy on honing down your niche and messaging?

After all, the smart brands and marketers looking to work with influencers today aren't necessarily looking for social influencers with massive followings (although it does help); they are looking for influencers with a tribe that is active and motivated.

What this means for you (especially if you have a small to medium sized tribe) is that as long as you can pick a subject matter and gain a vast amount of knowledge and credibility on it within your tribe, brands will start flocking to you.

Crafting the right message is about testing.

As hard as this might be to grasp, your tribe doesn't really care about you or your goals. They care about the things that matter to them. Often what your brand values won't matter to the audience you're trying to grow. That's why you need to craft your message through a series of test experiments where you ask your community what problems they face. Then it's up to you to figure out how to help them solve those problems.

If you do this right, you'll find you have more than 10 different messages or solutions. Start with choosing two that really excite you and come up with various strategies for communicating each one. Videos, blog posts, testimonials, success stories, pictures are all great ways of expressing your message.

From there, run tests to see which message and method gain more traction in the growing community. The more you learn what your tribe cares about, the greater impact and scale your messaging will have.

It will also make it easier for the brands that are a perfect fit for you to spot you. This level of clarity makes creating your pitch easy too, and we all know when the focus is placed on delivering what the audience wants, selling happens naturally.

Remember not every message you try will work. You might end up creating and testing 20 messages before you find one that hits a home run. The important thing is to keep testing and be mindful of the fact that tweaking is necessary when moving from one platform to the next. The same message that works well on Facebook may not do as well on Twitter. Learn to adjust accordingly. Once you've crafted a message that represents your brand well and aligns with your audience, you're ready to start selling products and services that resonate with your tribe.

Chapter 04: The Magic Of Great Content Creation

Original high-quality content is a crucial aspect of any successful influencer business. It is a core tool for your entire business. That's why you need to take the necessary measure to ensure your content is successful and trustworthy.

In this chapter, we dive into different aspects of content creation and how to set yourself up for success. But before that, let's draw a line in the sand here so you can stop making the grievous mistake of comparing yourself to influencers who are walking a different path. You see not all influencers are the same and it's time you make your stand.

Two kinds of online influencers, which side will you pick?

A twenty-two-year-old posted on her Instagram feed an image of herself and one of the Kardashian twins. You know the one who is super famous on Instagram? And on her captions she asked in disappointment - how is it that I'm still not as famous as the Kardashians after 2 years of daily posting?

It's easy for an outsider like me to get judgmental and call her silly. But in truth, the girl is just misinformed. She still doesn't realize what I am about to teach you. There are two main classes of influencers online today.

The first group is the one I call celebrity influencers. These are the Mega influencers with over a million followers. The Kardashians are a good example. People just want to follow them everywhere and see what they eat, where they sleep etc. They are famous for being famous. Whether or not they post something meaningful and inspiring people continue to flock around them. Actors, athletes like Cristiano Ronaldo, artists and other social media superstars with the highest reach on the influencer spectrum also fall into this category. Their influencer is driven by their celebrity status. When it comes to resonance and driving actions on behalf of a brand, they are actually scoring the lowest in terms of return on investment. So before you start getting jealous of a Kardashian and the fact that you have no way of getting a million followers, let's look at your other option.

The second group is the one I call content creating influencers. These are often macro-influencers. They are usually self-made individuals who produce amazing content consistently that's high quality and over time build a following. Think of people like Gary Vee and Tai Lopez if you really want an example. They've chosen certain subject matters and consistently push out inspiring, educative, entertaining and motivational content causing people to flock around them too. A journalist is also a content producer, and so is a blogger, analyst, author, etc. Macro-influencers usually have between 10,000 - 1 million followers and drive 5% - 25% engagement per post. They have the highest topical relevance on the spectrum and tend to be super niched down in categories like fashion, business, and lifestyle.

Hidden within this group of influencers is a smaller subset that is quickly gaining recognition as "micro-influencers."

A micro-influencer is like a mini version of a macro-influencer. Usually, these individuals are everyday consumers or employees who have between 500 - 10,000 followers and they actually have the highest brand relevance and resonance on the spectrum of influencers believe it or not. A micro influencer drives 25%-50% engagement per post, and because personal experience and relationship building within their networks drive their influence, they are quickly becoming some of the highest paid influencers.

The question is which side do you want to be on?

While anyone can produce content, not everyone can create amazing content that turns him or her into an influencer at whatever scale. Influential content is widely read, liked, commented on and shared. As a content creator, you don't need to have a large tribe to do well. What you need is to be seen as a credible authority on that topic and somewhat of an expert. You also need to be relatable. Many beauty influencers are relatable girls who consistently keep their audiences entertained, informed and inspired. So if like that twenty-two-year-old girl you're frustrated by the lack of fame, stop and re-assess your goals. Make a definite decision on whether you want to be on the side of mega influencers (the painful path to success) or on the side of macro and micro influencers.

Keep in mind that people like the Kardashians have a more massive empire they are building as a family all managed by their mom who is the key behind it all. And you're probably just a one man or one-woman show starting from scratch. The fame might eventually come, but don't waste your energy on wishful thinking. Pick a side that you know is the level ground where you can utilize all the resources available to you and create a meaningful community.

Aside from knowing where you stand as an influencer, it's also important to be strategic about this content you're creating. It's great that you're determined to put out world-class content, but how will you manage it all?

How will you ensure you're always consistent, on time and in alignment with your brand identity and messaging? The simple solution is to document your content strategy.

Documenting your content strategy

Your content strategy can be a few pages long or the size of a small book. It all depends on how detailed you want to be. But there's no escaping the fact that if you truly want to run a successful business, you need one. A documented strategy will help guide your decision-making. It will make it easier for you to visualize your entire ecosystem. It will also keep you accountable as you go through the planning, scheduling, publishing, and distribution of the actual content.

Many moving parts make up a content strategy, and it should be crafted around your specific needs and objectives. I encourage you not to abide by a rigid template. So rather than attempt to give you a one size fits all, let me outline what your document should include and then you can build upon and customize it to meet your needs.

• Current state

Make an assessment of your existing content as well as some insights into your competitor's content. Include the following:

Personas

Content Inventory

Competitive analysis

Gap analysis

Content audit

• Future of your content

This is where you gain clarity on where you want your content to take you and the various channels you will use to get there. Some of these places include:

Onsite content such as your landing pages, homepage, blog, etc.

Offsite content such as social media, emails etc.

• The content eco-system

You want to be able to create an environment in which the content is created. This also includes the way your content shall be governed adhering to your branding efforts. Some of these elements include an editorial calendar, brand voice and style guidelines as well as workflow analysis.

These steps might be a great starting point.

Step One: Document your discovery phase

This is the phase where you assess both the present and future of your content. It's where you ask yourself "why" you're doing what you're doing and the purpose this content should serve to help you express that why. After going through the various exercises in this book, it should be easy for you to identify your content objectives.

1. What task do you want the content to accomplish?

2. What behaviors do you want to influence with your content?

3. What are the goals, fears, and motivator of the audience you want to reach with your content?

4. Who are their heroes? What about their enemies?

5. Are there any content gaps that need to be filled?

6. Does your mix of channels make sense given your goals?

7. What content is currently working and what isn't?

Step Two: Document your content program

After going through step one, you should have a clear understanding of what to prioritize as you launch and feel free to tweak things as you go. This is always a continuous process. The elements that must be included in this phase are:

1. Your methodology for measuring.

This is what will inform your success at each stage of your business growth. Decide on the KPIs (Key Performance Indicators) that matter to you. Make sure they are specific, and all connect back to your goals.

2. Journey mapping

Outline the journey your leads and audience go through before they are ready to purchase something. How will your prospects be nudged along this journey? Are there signals to help you figure out which stage someone is in and can you create a particular technique to help move them along and have them ready to take action when you do make an offer? At what point will you start monetizing the audience?

3. Messaging

How is your content supporting your brand messaging? Which messages are currently relevant to the goals you want to reach? Will key messages resonate with all audiences or do you need to segment and personalize things more?

4. Channel opportunities

Take a look at all the channels and strategies you use (paid and organic) to get your audience to gather some audience insights. If you don't yet have any data, it's still worthwhile asking yourself these questions. How will you reach your audience? What will your mix of channels be?

5. Storytelling opportunities

Although many people consider this to be optional, as a social media influencer, it's crucial. Stories are what emotionally engage humans, and you need to make them a priority. You need a storytelling framework that helps you build content pillars and supports your goals.

6. SEO and Keyword planning

SEO is highly beneficial for content marketing although it's a more long-term strategy. Not all social media influencers care about SEO and keyword planning, but if you do want to use this as part of your strategy, some of the questions to answer are: How will you optimize content around keywords? What are the keywords you want to dominate? Are your publishing platforms optimized for SEO?

7.Editorial calendar

The editorial calendar will help you decide on things like, how often you will publish, how much content you'll put out daily and how you'll organize your campaigns. What formats will you create? Is your calendar aligned to the "life calendar" of your target personas? How will you publish and promote (and repurpose) each piece of content?

8. Budget Allocation

This is a huge benefit of creating a documented strategy because as you plan ahead of time, you can figure out ways of getting the most value out of your content and giving it the biggest reach. This is where the conversation on advertising comes into play. Figure out if you will use any paid ads to grow your audience and if so, work your way backward from your marketing goals to estimate the budget you'll allocate for this.

9. Outsourcing

If you need to expand and get a team, outsourcing and getting an extra hand to help complete a project might be a great way to go. In such cases, do your due diligence first to make sure you're bringing in the right creative partners and add this to your documented strategy.

10. Tools and resources

It's imperative to have the right tools to help you execute on your publishing and distribution. Although there are many bells and whistles on the web today and all kinds of software apps, you only need a handful to execute your vision well. Don't fall into the trap of buying something just because it looks good. Here are some of the resources I recommend checking out. Some are free others require monthly paid memberships.

Tools for Social media content publishing: Hootsuite and Buffer.

Platforms for blogging: Wordpress and Medium.

Tools for Analytics: Google Analytics, and Moz.

Software for Email marketing and relationship building outside social media platforms: Convertkit, Aweber, and Hubspot.

Tools for Social Monitoring: Meltwater, Trendkite

An editorial calendar and publishing tool: Coschedule

Tools for creating fast landing pages: Leadpages and Clickfunnels.

How to fuel your brand

Above and beyond creating amazing content consistently for your growing audience, you also need to find other ways of increasing your exposure. You need to find creative ways of positioning yourself as a transparent, energized influencer in the eyes of both your audience and brands looking to work with influencers. Every successful influencer needs extra fuel to keep his or her influence burning strong, and it's your job to figure out what will fuel you and your brand.

It may not be easy to push out as much content as many gurus suggest especially when just starting out and running everything on your own, but there specific creative ideas you can leverage to maximize brand reach.

One of the best ways to do this is through guest posting and creating relevant content for magazines and websites that speak on your topic. Since you're already a content creator, why not leverage your magical content by sharing it out to highly trafficked sites and magazines?

You'll get more brand recognition, build credibility and attract new people into your world. It can also open up opportunities for companies to find you or at least see your authority on your chosen niche.

You can also leverage user-generated content to continue fuelling your brand's growth and credibility. We all know that kind words from a customer are far more likely to be persuasive than your own recommendations. The more your tribe praises you, the more others will want to follow you and the more attractive you will be for high paying brands. Besides, this type of content (if published and placed in all the right places on your social channels) can continue to fuel your brand's overall content production.

Another thing to test out would be collaborations with peers in the same industry. This can be an Instagram takeover or a joint Facebook Live or any other type of collaboration where you get to be in front of a new audience, and you give your audience a chance to receive fresh new content from someone in a similar space. It also demonstrates your generosity and builds a lot of goodwill.

You and you alone are responsible for making this business work. As an influencer, you always need to have attractive, fresh content that draws more of your tribe in. You need to continually keep the fire burning by employing as many creative methods as you can conjure. Think outside the box, test out different things, and keep crafting your message and share news ideas on your chosen niche. You also need to radiate excitement in the work that you do and the tribe you're nurturing. Brands want to work with influencers who are motivated, thrilled about their products and excited to be partnering.

That energy is something you learn to generate as you create and publish your own content.

Testing, testing, and more social testing

I am adding on this extra piece before jumping into the more technical aspects of growing your brand as a social media influencer because I feel it's one that few influencers learn early enough.

The world of social media marketing is dynamic, and every audience is different. What works for one tribe on a particular platform may not work on a different platform. The best advice I can give you as you start growing is to make sure you are always testing and measuring all your campaigns and social media efforts.

Don't just publish for the sake of it. As I said before, each post needs to have a purpose and tied together with that purpose is a goal that you're moving toward. Measuring your success is therefore paramount. And the more you can test different tactics and strategies out, the faster you can know what works for you. So some of the low hanging fruits that you can start testing even as a novice include:

Testing the time of day that gets you the best audience reactions. Depending on the platforms you use, test out different times. Use tools within Twitter, Facebook Instagram, and the other social platforms to figure out when your audience is most active on the platform.

Testing the posts that get the most engagement. This is also super easy to implement. When you're on Facebook, which types of images work best? Is it just a single image or two or three images? What about links?

I have actually found that using multiple images (at least 2) per post gets more engagement on my page. Now go to the other platforms and carry out this simple test.

A lot of these tests will be done manually, and it might have a learning curve, especially if you're also testing emails, landing pages, etc. But with a little practice, you'll keep getting better. As you run tests be sure only to make one change at a time. If you change multiple things at once, it will be hard to know what made things better. So for example, if you're testing for Facebook posts and you're not sure if multiple images and links work, test one at a time. First post with a change in the number of images. Use two instead of one, and leave everything else as usual. Once you figure out whether it's working or not, you can move on to testing the removal of the link.

Remember, just because you've tested an idea and found that it worked in a particular way doesn't mean that it will always work. The algorithms are ever changing on social media so yes; keep doing what works until it doesn't. Then give yourself permission to continue testing and even retesting old tactics that failed in the past. Because you never know, though it failed in the past, this time around it might just work. As long as that's the kind of attitude you have, you'll always win on social media.

Key highlights from this section:

• Instead of trying to build a following, focus on building a tribe. See your people as humans under your care and serve them from the heart. Find a way to nurture your tribe online and offline.

• Use storytelling to connect your story, the products you promote and the interests of your tribe. The more they can relate to your story and connect it with their own journey, the more relevant your brand becomes.

• Lead with your passion and interests and find a topic that you are willing to master and share with your community.

• Be creative with your content, make sure it's useful, unique and on topic. When it comes to your brand messaging, give yourself permission to let it evolve. Run tests and experimentations with the ideas you have and gain feedback and data from your tribe so you can adjust it accordingly.

• Develop a simple, concise elevator pitch for your brand using the steps outlined.

• Pick a niche that has some competition, where there are fellow influencers in the same niche and where the audience is large enough and has spending power. Otherwise, you will have a hard time getting well-paying companies to hire your brand.

• You can choose to struggle your way into stardom and hope to become a mega influencer as a result of gaining celebrity status, or you can choose to join the group of content creators and become a macro-influencer or a micro-influencer.

• To create magical content that captivates your audience, you need a plan, a lot of research and a document outlining your project so you can easily create, manage and publish content consistently.

• Leverage the tools and technology that help you organize, publish, promote and distribute your content once you go through the steps outlined in this section.

• Pick one or two tactics to increase your brand exposure. The bigger the team, the more tactics you can implement simultaneously. When starting out alone or with a small team decide on one or two, whether that's paid advertising, guest blogging or any of the other suggested ideas to make sure you are giving your brand enough exposure online.

• Test and measure all the different strategies and tactics you choose to implement in your brand. The more you do, the more you'll know what works for you and what needs improvement. This is the best way to grow and scale your business.

Section Three:

" As long as I get to do my thing and someone wants to write me a check for it, I'm all about it."

- Mike Perry, Broad City Designer

Chapter 05: Packaging and Growing Your Brand

In this section, we are going to get really technical and break down uncomplicated ways you can start packaging yourself and growing your brand so that it starts becoming an income earner.

But before you can package anything, you need to have a brand identity and a growing audience. Let's talk more about that here.

A logo, a slogan, and a website are all cool, but they don't make your brand. Branding isn't something static; it's dynamic, progressive and is controlled by both you and your audience. The truth is you can do everything in your power to build your brand, but ultimately, your audience will perceive you in their mind as they choose to and there isn't much you can do about that. But what you can do is influence that perception as much as possible.

I like to think of this as helping your audience choose the right placement spot for you in their mind. To aid in this lifelong feat, there are few questions I encourage you to ask yourself as you grow and scale the business continually.

1. Who are my ideal clients (both paying and non-paying)?

2. What type of clients do I want to have?

3. What is my value proposition? Is it relevant to my audience?

4. When people think about my brand, what are the feelings and associations I want them to have?

5. What kind of personality will my brand have?

6. What are the emotional benefits that only I can deliver to my audience?

7. What brands do I admire?

8. What are my brand colors?

9. What fonts will I use in my communications?

10. How can I streamline my visual content?

11. What is my audience's "Language"?

12. What impact do I want my brand to have in the world?

How to quickly grow an engaged audience organically

While you can put some advertising budget aside to help expand your reach and brand awareness, I encourage you to focus first on organic growth. You don't want to pay for people to follow you. You can pay for more people to become aware of your content (boosting content) but let the actual following grow as a natural consequence of them discovering how amazing your content is. And since we've talked extensively about creating great content in the previous section, I'm going to assume you're ready for takeoff at this point.

I know it can get frustrating when starting out because it seems like you're just talking to yourself and no one seems interested but take comfort, we all start from there. Even the great Gary Vee said it took a lot of time to build engagement on his Twitter and YouTube channels and look at him today. I can't tell you how long it will take for you to start seeing massive participation in your community, but

I can share tips that will ensure you're on the right track.

Tip #1: Incorporate a lot of video content

Videos are the most consumed type of content in today's digital world. In February 2017, Facebook CEO Mark Zuckerberg said, " I see video as a megatrend." He was so right. There's an explosion of growth in video on social media that is still predicted to continue rising. Views of branded video content increased 99% on YouTube and 258% on Facebook between 2016 and 2017 according to wyzowl. And that was just the beginning. On Twitter, a video tweet is 6X more likely to be retweeted than a photo tweet. Those are really huge numbers, and they keep growing each year.

All this to say, you need to be producing as much video content as you can.

Many of the social platforms like LinkedIn and Facebook push out video content more than other types of content and give more exposure to people who post videos regularly. If you didn't include video into your strategy, now is the time to go hard and invest heavily in video production. People like Gary Vee have built entire businesses leveraging mostly video content. You can do the same too. If you have a smartphone, you've got everything you need to get started.

Tip #2. Use hashtags often
This is a quick and essential part of quickly growing an engaged audience. It will expose your posts to new eyes and make it easier for

people who don't know your brand to find and follow you. Make sure to do some research and find the right hashtags that will lead to long-term longevity. Although using a popular hashtag is a nice short-term solution, it may not always be the best idea because you might end up attracting generic people who aren't a perfect fit.

Tip #3. Engage with everyone

I've seen a lot of newbies skipping this part, and it hurts their growth. When you start posting, you need to engage with everyone who reacts to your content. It doesn't matter whether you consider them the right fit for your audience or not, if someone has taken the time to look at your content and engage, they deserve acknowledgment. Let everyone who interacts with your content know that you are human, that you care, that you are reading their responses and listening to what they want. The more people get used to this, the more they will engage whenever you post something because all humans want to be seen and heard. Use this to your brands' advantage.

Tip #4. Provide an irresistible benefit for your growing audience

Everyone is tuned into the WIIFM radio station. WIIFM (What's in it for me) broadcasts the best tunes, and when you align your brand and platform with this station, you're destined to win. People who find you online have only one question running through their minds "what's in it for me?"

If you can offer something beneficial to them right off the bat, something designed to draw them deeper into your world while at the same time adding some value in their life, you'll be building trust and a captivated audience. Come from a place of abundance. Be generous with your gift and offer something that is super relevant to the audience you're nurturing while still remaining aligned with your overall goals.

Tip #5: Gamify the process

People love to respond to quizzes and questions. Using games (if it aligns with your personality and brand style) can be a great way to grow a following quickly. You can quickly build up followers and engagement on your platform.

You and I both know being an influencer is a full-time gig that requires you to wear many different hats including content creation, photography, graphics designing, community management, and the list goes on and on. Since you're going to put this much effort into it, having an idea of how to package yourself so you can be equipped to monetize at the right time is essential.

Why do you need to consider packaging your services?

As an influencer, brands will often come to you knowing they want results, but they may not be sure how you can actually help them or worse still, they might be going in the direction that won't yield optimum results and show a high ROI, which as we know will not bode well for you. Because we know it's your reputation at stake when you chose to collaborate with a brand, it is useful to start having an idea of the different ways you can best serve the companies you want to work with.

If potential clients can see your services and how you can help them or how you've helped other brands in the past, they can start having a clear picture of the best way to collaborate with you. It's one thing for a company to make assumptions about what they need from an influencer. It's another to look at a package you've created and have them realize "yes that's exactly what we need!" Or at least pave the way for a customized service that resonates with both parties.

Therefore your job in this section is to make sure you learn to package your offers concisely and attractively for the potential companies you desire to work with. Packing your services makes it easier for your prospects to process information about you and why they should collaborate with you. It makes the decision making process easier, reduces cognitive barriers and prompts them to buy-in to your offer.

Now it's time to decide what services you want to offer:

This can go as in-depth as you like, but I recommend starting easy. You already know the things you're passionate about, the brands that you want to work with, etc. Think along the lines of what these brands are most interested in getting across to their ideal consumers and then reverse engineer it back to you and your brand.

You might have to do some research on this and even study what other influencers in your niche are doing or check out the type of marketing the brands you wish to work with are doing.

For example, if you want to work with a sustainable clothing brand, you can create a package that includes various types of content shared across multiple platforms each tweaked to match the different social platforms so the brand can get the most out of your collaboration. You might have another packaged offer that even includes some kind of interactive educational Livestream where you take people behind the scenes and share the story of the clothing brand freshly and uniquely.

There are many ways to approach this, but the beauty of having these packages is that you can focus on offering what you absolutely love doing. That will make pouring your energy into a campaign all the more enjoyable, and those brands that resonate with your way of communicating online will quickly find you.

If there is a secret sauce to be leveraged in digital marketing, this is it!

What am I talking about?

Storytelling.

Your brand can stand out and differentiate itself easily if you integrate powerful storytelling techniques that have been proven to work. We all know the power of a great story. It's part of human nature to lean in and pay closer attention when a grand narrative is going on whether that's around a campfire, the dinner table, workshop, or over the phone. In today's world, brands like Netflix have exponentially taken over the entertainment scene because they found a way to leverage technology and place great stories in front of a hungry audience that craves uninterrupted storytelling. Creating a storybrand script that resonates with your audience and shows the human side of your business will go a long way in establishing you as a trusted expert.

Why should you focus on narratives and storytelling?

Well, first of all, it's the easiest way to make your brand relatable. Being relatable as an influencer is really important. So you need to have good relatable characters with personalities and interests. More importantly (especially for your story brand script) you need to have a common villain or conflict that unites you and your tribe.

You also need to make sure your stories have a beginning middle and an end with a pace that's easy to follow. If you open a loop, please make sure you close it before losing the attention of your audience.

Beginning - middle - end is a simple narrative arc that can be used in endless ways so let your creativity run wild as you start crafting the narratives that will help you script your brand's story and content.

There are many story scripts you can create for yourself and your brand. Be flexible with the scripts and keep testing now angles to see what generates more positive reactions.

Consider sharing what you're currently working on, or a "behind the scenes" look at what it means to be an influencer and grow a thriving business. You can also share stories about your learning experience working with brands and what that process looks like. Whatever you choose to share, make sure it's in alignment with the overall mission of the brand. Always try to stay true to your messaging and the brand image you want the world to know.

Another great tip when it comes to leveraging storytelling is to make sure the story brand script is personal, relatable and client focused. Since your clients are both paying brands and the audience you're growing, make sure they take center stage of your brand's story. When starting out, focus more on the brand's story as it relates to your audience and let things unfold naturally. People don't by into brands; they buy into the story behind the brands. You - are what people buy into and that's what makes you influential.

Reinforce your brand's message and the things you stand for. Your tribe will feel more connected the more you share these types of content on social media. For example, if you want to become an influencer in the natural health products niche and you love Whole Foods then share information that portrays that message clearly. You can share healthy tips, food recipes, and ingredients that you get from Whole Foods, etc. Perhaps you had health issues that led to this transformation, and Whole Foods played a role in helping you heal and change your eating habits. As you share that story, make sure each piece of content no matter how small is used to reinforce the story you want to communicate. As you do, your brand builds credibility and relatability. It also makes your content super relevant to a specific audience.

How to use narratives on your social platforms:

I know you might be thinking " storytelling sounds excellent and I can see that happening on my website or blog but is it efficient on social platforms?

Absolutely. Let me prove it to you by sharing a few examples on some of the social channels.

You can work narratives into your Facebook posts by turning your status updates into little blog posts. Many savvy personal brands are actually starting to do this. Authors are a great example of individuals who are regularly posting narratives on their Facebook pages. Author Anne Lammott is worth checking out. On her Facebook page, she shares stories about herself and the things that are happening around her, and it's drawing extensive comments and likes.

You can also work digital storytelling into your Instagram posts by sharing a simple narrative on your captions as you post the image. Gather inspiration from big brands like Airbnb who have mastered this art of sharing stories about each location they post. This same narrative technique can be used across almost any social network you can think of.

Can you see how simple and fun this can be if you think outside the standard way of doing things?

Most people just think about cat videos or making offers on social media. These cannot be your staple form of content if you want to stand out and actually grow.

Building a team

When is the right time for you to start building a team around your business?

There is no rigid right answer to this. Few people have the bandwidth to simultaneously cover all the necessary business areas without going insane. Whether you start off alone or with a team, you'll soon realize it takes a working team to grow a thriving business.

Many experts encourage outsourcing and putting a team together from day one. This, of course, depends a lot on your objectives, your core competencies and whether or not you have funds to support having extra people around.

In today's digital world, having a team doesn't need to be stressful and costly. If you know how to pick the right individuals, you can assemble talented freelancers and contractors who can work with you remotely. Platforms such as Upwork, Fiverr and others are great for sourcing talent. But of course, you need to be able to attract and retain the right people.

When it comes to hiring an agent, a virtual assistant and all those other roles that meant to aid you to grow and scale the business, there is also no definite time for you bring them on. But I would say these types or roles become more important for your business once you actually have an audience and some forward momentum.

Regardless of when you choose to assemble your team, you'll still need to put in the necessary work because it won't be easy. At times, building a team can be as critical and as difficult as building your brand. Finding the right team doesn't just happen overnight, and if you get a team that doesn't work well together, it doesn't matter how epic your brand is, you'll have a hard time achieving your goals.

A key take away point to include here is also about choosing your agent. Many brands and advertising companies have expressed their disappointment when having to work with an agent who doesn't represent an influencer well. If you get to a point where you choose to work with an agent, make sure they are amplifying your success not hindering it. You need someone who will represent you well in front of your paying prospects. Your agent and everyone who gains access to your paying and non-paying clients must be in alignment with your values and the core mission that you serve.

A few general pointers might go a long way in helping you envision and bring together the right people that will enable you to focus on doing more of what you love.

One. Make sure you take the time to define your business culture.

A great team begins with you. Find the right people in the different areas you need help with who resonate with you and the culture you want to nurture. It might seem like a good idea to go for cheap or free interns and family members, but if these people aren't aligned with your thinking and vision, things will crumble pretty fast.

Two. Each team member that comes on board must choose to be proactive and contribute as best they can.

They need to fully step into their role, bring out the best in others and collaborate across their areas of expertise to deliver on the shared objective of your brand. It will be your job to measure each person's performance and results.

Three. Foster stable relationships within the team and stay focused on what matters.

If there is bad energy, lack of synergy and poor communication among the team members, it will dilute the impact and performance of the team. It's impossible for people to be productive and focus on high-quality execution when distracted by petty issues and poor relationships with one another, so I recommend clearly communicating the purpose of coming together and making sure people actually enjoy working together.

Four. Energize your team around the shared purpose of your brand, the community and what you want to achieve ultimately.

As an influencer your ability to nurture and motivate people is indispensable. That goes for the community you're growing as well as the team working in the background with you. The team can only help you build a successful social media business when the members feel appreciated, heard and valued. The more open-minded and receptive they are to your vision of the changing world and your guidance the higher your success will be. This is, therefore, no time for you to be wasting energy "protecting" yourself or "micro-managing" people because you lack faith in their ability to execute. Doing so will just dissipate the energy you could be using to build the necessary connections and bonds that lead to a successful team.

Five. Mobilize hearts and mind by converting your vision into milestones

Every new business team has a big job to do and lots of barriers, obstacles, swirling priorities, and seemingly impossible deadlines. Too many influencers make the mistake of just throwing a bunch of people together with no proper vision, clear strategy and old knowledge on how to work with others. Don't make this same mistake.

Empower your team and help them create action plans for delivering exceptional results in their assigned roles. Equip your team members with the right tools, education, and resources that enable them to ask the type of questions that lead to positive results. Let them bring innovative ideas and creativity. The more they can participate in this journey with you the more invested with will be physically, mentally and spiritually.

Assembling a team may or may not be on your immediate to do list but at some point on this journey, you will need to start forming one. When you do, keep these things in mind because getting an average team will only lead to mediocre results. You need a team that is epic to help exponentially grow and scale your brand.

Getting on the right side of the law

Even as a novice working your way up into stardom, it's essential to become aware of the rules around influencer marketing. As with any business, there are laws and regulations in place for most countries, though not all.

Definitely, check in with local authorities to figure out what the law requires you to adhere to as a social media influencer.

In the United States, for example, the Federal Trade Commission (FTC) has a set of guidelines that you must read and implement from the get-go. Failure to do so can result in some pretty agonizing consequences.

Take for example the story of Lord & Taylor's "Paisley Dress Campaign." They worked with fifty fashionistas who are Instagram influencers. Each fashionista posted pictures of the dress on their community reaching 11.4 million individual Instagram users and led to 328,000 engagements. This was a great success for the campaign of course, but there was just one problem. The influencers did not disclose that they were paid thousands of dollars each to post a photo of themselves wearing the dress on Instagram and other social media sites.

As a result, the FTC had to take legal action on the retail company. You don't want to find yourself in such a situation so please learn everything you can about laws and regulations before accepting a dollar from any company.

You might be thinking that you're "too small" to get in the crosshairs of the FTC because they only focus on big-money advertisements like a hundred thousand dollar commercials, right?

Wrong. They actually monitor social media just as carefully as any other advertising platforms. I mean yes, social media is massive, and the sheer volume of content is perhaps impossible at this time to monitor each and every single one, but still, you shouldn't try the sneaky approach. It's a huge risk and ethically speaking it's just not right. Better to just adhere to the moral so that as you grow, it becomes part of your standard level of performance online.

The other all-important reason to stay on the right side of the law with your sponsored ads and endorsements is that the more transparent you are with your tribe, the more successful your campaigns will be long-term because you'll never risk losing the trust of your audience. They will know when you're sponsoring a brand and when you're generously sharing unpaid content. This trust is priceless because it leads to that perception of authenticity. If your audience loses confidence in you and thinks you're sneaky or manipulative, it can almost be impossible to gain it back. So set yourself up for success and be open about the brands you work with.

Here are several FTC guidelines to help you get started:

• Sponsored social media posts should include clear disclosures such as "#sponsored," "#paid" or "#ad" before any links leading back to a brand's landing page.

• Endorsers shouldn't talk about their experience with a product or service if they haven't actually tried it, or used it as they say.

• If an endorser is paid to review a product but had a horrible experience, they can't say that it was wonderful.

•In a blog post, the disclosure statement must come before the affiliate link and above the "fold" or "scroll."

•On image-only platforms, disclosure should be over the picture in a clear font that contrasts sharply with the background.

•For videos and audio content, there must be either an audible verbal disclosure at the start or a written declaration on a clearly legible title card at the beginning of the video.

•Make sure influencers don't use tiny fonts or pale colors to disguise sponsorship disclosure.

- Ensure influencers disclose sponsorship as close to the beginning of the content as possible.

I recommend you read through the entire FTC guidelines thoroughly to avoid undesirable situations and clearly and conspicuously disclose the business relationship with a brand whenever you post something.

Chapter 06: Marketing and Advertising

The most effective way to grow a community of super fans and exponentially grow your influencer brand is to learn how to market your brand authentically.

Now, it bears clarifying that marketing and advertising are not one and the same. In case you get confused by these terms, let's do a brief description of each term.

Marketing can be described as the big umbrella that covers every touch point you make with a prospect or client (paying and non-paying). Assistant professor of marketing for the Gabelli School of Business at Roger Williams University, Kathleen Micken defines marketing as everything an organization does to facilitate an exchange between itself, and it's clients.

In your case, your organization is your brand, and your clients are both the companies you want to work with as well as the tribe you nurture.

Advertising is just one piece of your marketing puzzle. It is actually a subset of marketing; an activity that comes with a hard dollar cost attached. When starting out you may or may not include advertising into your marketing plan, but marketing itself is not optional. Unless you know how to market yourself to both types of clients, you don't stand a chance at becoming a highly paid social media influencer.

- The two types of clients you need to serve with excellence

If you want to do well and get paid thousands of dollars each month as an influencer, you must do a good job attracting and serving the two clients that determine how wealthy you can be in your space.

The first type of client is your audience or tribe.

These are your followers or the individuals that form your tribe. The more known, trustworthy and credible you become the more influential and desirable you become to your second type of client. When building your business, your followers are your first clients, and even though they don't spend money on you, their attention is the most important investment they can make with you.

The more you have their attention and influence their behavior, the more money you can hope to make. Why?

Because in the influencer marketing world, money follows attention.

So you want to make sure all your marketing plans are well laid out to ensure that every touch point where your client interacts with you, your content and brand is an experience that keeps him or her captivated.

The second type of client is the potential company or brand that could pay you to partner up with them.

This is where influencer marketing comes into play. And with stats like the ones I am about to share, you should be very thrilled to grow your brand because the potential to earn a wealthy living are virtually unlimited at this point.

• Around 40% of people reported that they purchased a product online after seeing it used by an influencer on YouTube, Twitter or Instagram. Twitter says users now trust social media influencers nearly as much as a friend or neighbor.

• According to a study by Tomson, influencer marketing yields a $6.50 return on investment for every dollar spent.

• When it comes to millennials, 33% of them say they trust blog reviews for their purchases, but only 1% of them believe traditional advertisements.

It's no wonder influencer marketing is becoming a priority for brands. And they are looking for influencers with both large and small followings. Remember the stats I shared about Macro and micro influencers? That's why choosing the side of micro-influencers is a better path to stardom for you especially if you don't have Kardashian money to fund your online activities.

What matters most for businesses interested in influencer marketing is the level of engagement a community has and how pleasant the relationship is between the influencer and the company. After all, if you don't do a great job helping a company reach its objectives, it's unlikely you'll be able to build long-term growth.

Bottom line. Marketing is going to be critical for you at every phase of your business growth, and you'll have to think of it as a two-sided coin. On the one hand, you need a plan that will help you nurture a fantastic audience. On the other hand, you need a program that will help you attract and retain high paying brands.

So far I have been sharing tips to help you attract and nurture an amazing community. Before moving on to section four where we dive deep into each of the platforms so you can set up shop and start implementing all these ideas, let me share tips on how you can market yourself and your brand better so that companies can quickly see the value of working with you.

Tips to marketing yourself and your brand in a noisy and competitive marketplace

• Stop trying to find the "right tactic" or "secret marketing sauce" and instead focus on the core message.

Your "WHY" is the main thing you should be focused on at all times. If you haven't watched Simon Sinek's video on YouTube (start with "Why"), I recommend you do that once you're done reading this.

You'll hear a lot of gurus making a fuss about where you put your call to action button, the color of your buttons on a landing page or the font that you use. And these are all great, however, getting lost in the tactics and logistics of marketing may actually do more harm to your brand as an influencer.

You are in the business of serving people. Focus more on why you want to serve as an influencer in your niche and how you make people feel whenever they interact with your content. Those feelings that your audience feels when interacting with you are what result in actions further down the line.

• Start thinking about this audience you're growing as human beings not a means to an end.

The allure of becoming famous, making a lot of money and living a luxurious life can totally distract you from the significant aspect of wanting to be an influencer in the first place.

Being responsible for a community, for helping people feel like they matter and gaining their trust is a huge deal. You are dealing with human beings, not follower count or leads. Shift from that very limited mindset and start seeing yourself as a steward of something much bigger than yourself and your marketing will sparkle because you'll be creating it from the heart.

• Only do, say, create and advocate for things you honestly feel connected to.

I say this because so many influencers make decisions based on the money they could make. They end up saying and doing things they don't feel connected to which of course flops because their audience also fails to connect and take action.

Your community has the same BS meter that you have, and they know when you're not being genuine about a product or topic. If you're following a script that doesn't feel right for your brand or forcing yourself to follow marketing tricks that gurus have said work, your clients will both pick up on this "fake energy."

Think of all the marketing tools, resources, and tactics as suggestions because in truth no one really knows what will work best for you. Marketing is about testing things out. Anyone who tells you any different is just sabotaging your success.

What works for one influencer in your same niche may not work for you because you are a unique individual and your personality is what makes all the difference in this industry. So blindly following what others say isn't something I recommend. Learn as much as you can and be willing to experiment, but at the end of the day, always follow your gut and what feels right for you and your community.

• Be prepared to go the extra mile

Jay Abraham said in an interview that it's arrogant to think that the market should just come and find you. In other words, he was saying you can't just sit there and wait for your tribe to happen or for brands to show up on your DM with invitations for partnerships.

To build your brand, you must market yourself and your brand. You must work diligently and advocate for yourself. Find ways to be published in relevant magazines and website, do press releases, pitch every brand you can possibly think of and do your best to build relationships with fellow influencers who already have an audience you can add value to. Be extremely active on all the relevant social platforms that you wish to dominate and offer your time to teach, share insights or even create content that can be cross-promoted. Your lack of imagination and creativity is the only limitation here. You can market your brand in so many ways and get in front of new people each and every week, but you must be willing to put in the time and effort.

Without consistent effort in your marketing, you won't become a great marketer. And as a social media influencer, marketing is where you shine. The more you can develop this skill and learn to gain attention even without advertising budgets, the more valuable you become as an influencer. Of course, you can also add in layers of advertising to boost the content you create, increase reach and raise brand awareness for yourself, but these require extra funds and a learning curve that this book doesn't get into.

Marketing is a core component of your success as an influencer, and although I have barely scratched the surface here, you now have enough knowledge to get your brand up and running. It's time to set up shop on the platforms you want to dominate.

Key highlights from this section:

• You need to create a brand identity that resonates with your values as well as the tribe you want to nurture.

• Package your services so that it's easier for your prospects to process information about you, your brand, the type of audience you serve and why they should collaborate with you.

• Use the power of storytelling to stand out and differentiate yourself from the rest of the influencers in your niche. This is one of the most effective ways to connect with your audience, gain their trust and grow your brand.

- At some point on this journey, you will need to start putting together a team. This will require you to prep yourself beforehand and get clear on the culture you wish to cultivate as well as the type of people you want to have working with you. An average team will yield average results; a great team that enjoys working together and supports your mission wholeheartedly will help you exponentially scale your business.

- To stay in the goodwill of your growing tribe, social media platforms, and the FTC, remember to read and follow al influencer marketing guidelines. Maintain transparency and authenticity.

•Marketing and advertising is not one and the same thing. When starting out, advertising may be optional for you, but marketing is a must.

• You must serve your clients with excellence. Your tribe is your client, and so are the brands that pay you to endorse their products and services. They all deserve the best from you.

• Focus more on your "Why" and how you make your clients feel. The emotions that your clients experience when interacting with you are by far the determining factor of whether your brand will thrive and whether you will be positioned as an influencer in your niche.

• You are a steward and nurture of your community. The people that follow you and perceive you as an influencer deserve your care, and you should treat every single person as an essential human being, not a lead or a means to an end.

• If you BS your audience they will feel it and lose faith in you and your brand. As the FTC guidelines put it, if you use something and it wasn't fantastic, don't try to "fake it" just because you're getting paid. The reason your community trusts you and takes on your recommendation is that they believe you will protect them from false claims and direct them towards truth and the things that will actually improve their lives.

• Marketing is a skill set that you can only get better at through practice. Learn as much as you can, test and experiment and enjoy the process of figuring out what works for you and what doesn't. At the end of the day, always go back to your gut and your "why."

• Marketing yourself is a must. And it is hard work that requires consistent effort. So roll up your sleeves and do the work. Stay on your own lane, avoid distractions, keep your priorities straight and expect that soon enough the market place will recognize the value you bring as long as you keep bringing it.

Section Four:

" People influence people. Nothing influences people more than a recommendation from a trusted friend. A trusted referral influences people more than the best broadcast message. A trusted friend is the Holy Grail of advertising.

- Mark Zuckerberg

Chapter 07: The Platforms

Now that you have your niche chosen, your business and content strategy ready, it's time to learn more about the social platforms that could make you a superstar. To become a highly paid social media influencer, you need to dominate one or more social channels, and this is the section that helps you choose the best fit for you.

If you want to enjoy a fraction of the influence and followership that people like PewDiePie or Jacksepticeye (self-made YouTubers) experience, then choosing your platform carefully is a must.

My recommendation is to start with one or two social platforms maximum. Strive for depth and mastery within your chosen platform rather than trying to be everywhere. If you try too much too soon and you don't have a team to support your growth you'll just dissipate your energy and resources. And you might not get the necessary traction to grow your tribe.

Brands aren't necessarily looking for an influencer who is big on all channels. Depending on their objectives, they might work with a relatively small influencer who dominates just one channel. So don't get so worked up about building multiple communities all at once. Establish yourself and your tribe on one platform and then expand as your influence grows.

Below I share with you everything you need to know about the leading social platforms where influencers are making money. Since this book is meant to take you from newbie to pro in the shortest timeframe possible, I intend to share as much relevant information about the channel and the subtle differences you need to be aware of as you set up your accounts as well as the different content types that have been proven to work. I even do my best to share some real-world examples of influencers in various niches so that you can get some extra inspiration for your niche. Be sure to customize this information to suit your needs and niche market.

Facebook

This social platform has dominated the world of socializing online. At the time of writing this, there are over 2.23 billion monthly active users globally and growing. Every second there are 20,000 people on Facebook, which means in just 18 minutes there are 11 million users actively using it. Talk about endless opportunity to grow your audience.

Facebook generates $1.4 million in revenue every hour. Most of their income does come from advertising, so when it comes to audience reach and brand awareness, they are certainly demonstrating that it is a pay to play arena.

66% of all millennials (15 - 34-year-olds) use Facebook. 31% of US senior citizens are on

Facebook and users spend an average of 21 minutes per day on Facebook.

How to set up your Facebook Fan page:

Step one: Fill out your necessary information and how you want to represent your personal brand.

Go   to https://www.facebook.com/pages/creation.
Once there you'll see two options - "Business or Brand" and "Community and Public Figure." Choose whichever feels congruent with your objectives and continue following the instructions provided. My suggestion is using the Business or Brand option. In the end, you will have shared some of your

information, and the page will start to populate.

Step two: Add a profile photo and cover photo

Facebook will prompt you to upload a profile image and cover photo or video.

The profile image dimensions are - 170 pixels wide by170 pixels tall.

This photo will appear as your icon every time you comment on a post or publish in the news feed. Ideally, you want to upload a good image of yourself rather than a logo.

The cover photo dimension is 820 pixels wide by 462 pixels tall. This appears across the top of your page and is a great opportunity to deliver a visual element that supports your branding, draws in attention and elicits emotion from your visitors.

According to Facebook, your cover image is displayed at different sizes on desktops and on smartphones, i.e., 820 pixels wide by 312 pixels tall on desktops and 640 pixels wide by 360 pixels tall on smartphones so if you want to use a single image that works for both my recommendation in that 820 x 462.

If you are feeling more adventurous try testing out a cover video instead of an image or a feature slideshow of images.

Step three: Finish filling out your information

Facebook will show you a few tips to complete your Facebook Page set up. You'll see a section right in the middle of your new Facebook page where you can click to "See All Page Tips," and it'll walk you through everything you need to do. Be creative about this. It forms part of the copywriting and messaging that represents your brand. All the details you fill in will appear on the About tab of your Facebook Page, and here you can add your origin story, awards, mission, etc.

Before moving on to the next step, I also want you to create a username for your page to make it easier for people to find your page. This will also give you a custom URL that you can share with others.

I also want you to add a prominent call to action by using the button that Facebook provides below the cover photo. It's a great opportunity for your new audience to take the next action and become part of your tribe.

Step Four: Customize your page

Go to Page settings, and you'll find a "Templates and Tabs" tabs. Here you can configure the look and feel of your Page. Tabs are fundamentally different sections of your Page such as your posts, photos, testimonial reviews, etc. You can decide which tabs you want on your Page and their order.

If you are going to have a Facebook Group (which I recommend if you want to be a Facebook Influencer), you can choose the template that allows you to highlight it. You can link it to your Facebook Page for more visibility.

Step Five: Publish your first post

Now it's time to add fresh new content to your new page. This can be a status update, a link, an image, a video, an event or a milestone. Adding content to your page consistently and regularly will make your page look all the more attractive to new visitors as they discover you.

And there you have it, your Facebook Fan Page is up and ready to deliver some amazing content to your new tribe and fans. It's time to start implementing the content strategy you decided on and work on growing that audience.

Most influencers who are active on Facebook also build a community using Facebook groups. But a common question I've gotten is "what's the difference between the two and do I really need one?

It's a tough one to give a simple answer to because both are quite popular. They aren't identical, and I would say, if you want more organic engagement (especially since the new algorithm took effect) it might be worthwhile having both. Let's detail some critical features of each.

Facebook page
• Has built-in analytics (Page Insights).
• Has a call-to-action button (CTA) where you can invite new visitors to Learn More, Sign Up, Book Now, etc. directly from the Facebook Page.
• You can like and comment as your Facebook Page.

• You can add apps and services to your Facebook Page so that your fans can easily order/purchase products, make a booking, get a quote and so on.

• You can boost your Facebook Page, Page posts and Events with Facebook ads.

Facebook Group:

• Has built-in analytics, which is a pretty new feature (Group Insights).

• You can set your Facebook group as exclusive and private (Closed or Secret).

• You can do group chatting with group members.

• Your members always receive notifications about new posts to the Group.

There are some best practices for Facebook posting that you may want to consider. I'll be sharing some of that once we help you set up your group. So let's jump into that.

How to set up your Facebook community:

Facebook groups are the place to connect with other like-minded people, and it's becoming increasingly crucial for a social media influencer to have if they want to cultivate a large community. Follow these steps to create your Facebook Group from within the Facebook Page you just created and start nurturing an engaged community.

Step one. Decide on your Facebook Group Name and privacy settings

All you need to do once you have a name is to click on "Group under the "Create" section at the bottom left sidebar on Facebook. You can also do it directly from your Facebook Page. Fill out the necessary info in the pop-up and hit create.

Step two: Fill out your Facebook Group's info

From your Group settings (you can locate this by clicking on the three-dots button below your cover photo), choose "Edit Group Settings."

• Add a cover photo.

Again, the dimensions I recommend for this is 820 pixels wide by 462 pixels tall. Make sure the photo aligns with your brand.

• Select a group type to help people understand what the group is about. Depending on how you want to position yourself, Facebook gives you several options to choose from.

• Create a descriptive copy to help your tribe understand what the group is about.

You have up to 3,000 characters for your group description so try to be as detailed as possible. And yes, you can use emojis here.

• Add tags to help your tribe find your group.

You can use up to five tags. Think it through and make sure these are keywords that connect your brand to the ideal audience. As you start typing Facebook will offer suggestions.

• Add your location if you want to attract more of a local audience.

By adding a location people who are interested in your topic or looking for a group in your local area will easily find you. You can also add multiple locations if you want.

• Customize your Facebook Group URL.

Use an easy to remember URL so that as you share your Facebook Group on other platforms or in network events and conferences, people will quickly find you. The maximum is 50 characters but the shorter it is, the better.

Step three. Add or invite friends and promote your Facebook Group

Head on over to the "Add Members" field on the right of your Facebook group and start asking more people to join your new Group.

To add a friend you can enter their name in the field, and he or she will automatically join the group without having to accept an invitation. If you want to invite a prospect or new customer just enter their email address. You can also add a personalized note on the invitation by clicking on the tiny blue icon on the right.

To share your new Facebook Group click the "Share" button just below your cover photo. This allows you to share on your timeline,

Messenger and Facebook Page. Don't forget to circulate this on other social platforms as well where you're growing fans.

Step Four. Set guidelines and moderate discussions

You can either write them in your group description like some people do or create and pin a post. You could even create a Facebook document. Include things such as the actions that are encouraged and those that should be avoided. Also, let your tribe know who the team members are and the respective roles in case they need support. I also recommend you edit your membership and posting settings so that you can moderate and be in control of all that happens within the Group. Go to "Group Settings" and set permissions for new membership and posting depending on what you feel comfortable with.

If you would like to learn more about new members as they join, you can ask them to fill up a short questionnaire. Ask up to three questions, and they'll have up to 250 characters to share a bit more about themselves.

One of the cool things about the Facebook Group platform is that you or your moderators can remove posts and comments on posts that violate the guidelines. And if you keep getting a member who continuously violates your group you can remove and block them from the Group entirely.

Using Facebook Groups to increase brand equity

Facebook groups are an excellent way for you to generate more engagement around your brand. To cultivate a group that is responsive and engaged, post regularly, have a strategy around the content you share within the group and keep checking the insights to inform your publishing strategy. I also suggest finding creative ways of running things like contests, giveaways and other types of events. In-person meet-ups are also a great way to build a meaningful connection with your community.

Most popular niches on Facebook:

If you're wondering whether your niche market would work well on this platform, here is a small list of some of the best performing niches.

- Fitness
- Dating
- Personal Development
- Make Money Online
- How To's
- Spirituality and Alternative Beliefs
- Sustainability
- Minimalism
- Green Energy
- Survival Niche (DIY)
- Sports
- Parenting
- Camping
- Real Estate
- Religion
- Digital Marketing
- Design

- Photography

- Videography

- Art

Best practices for growing your Facebook following:

1. Make sure your images are at least 180 pixels wide by 180 pixels tall, and the cover photo is 820 pixels wide by 312 pixels tall.

2. Leverage the power of Facebook Live. It's the best way to interact with viewers in real-time. Your followers will receive notifications whenever you go live so they'll know to tune in to receive your broadcast at just the right time.

3. The best time to post of Facebook according to collected research done by Coschedule on both mobile devices and desktop computers depends mostly on the type of audience you serve. No single answer fits everyone. So here are three slots to test out. 9:00 AM, when people are just going online for the first time or about to start working. 11:00 AM - 12:00 PM when people are taking their lunch break. 3:00 PM - 4:00 PM especially if you're growing your brand around software and education. The best days to post on Facebook are Thursday to Sunday.

4. Test out the different types of media content to see which one your tribe engages with the most on this channel. A video, single images, multiple images, blog posts with URL, native posts are all worth testing out until you find

what works, then keep creating more of the same.

5. Listen and improve as you create and publish content on this platform. The feedback you get from your followers should inform you of the direction the brand needs to take. Learn from your tribe and improve your brand as you engage directly with all your followers.

Instagram

At the time of writing this, Instagram has over 1 Billion monthly active users and is the second most engaged network after Facebook. 60% of its users log in daily, and the most significant demographic is aged between 18 - 24 years.

Although most of Instagram active users are under 35 years old, it still carries a substantial demographic that most brands want to target. It's no wonder most social media influencers want to be known on Instagram. The rewards of having a powerful tribe on Instagram can be very gratifying.

Some influencers claim to charge upwards of $25,000 for a single Instagram post. Influence

Central found that consumers actually rank Instagram influencers sixth place on their level of effectiveness when it comes to influencing purchases. It's definitely not an exaggeration to say your riches could be sitting on Instagram as we speak!

Now that you already have your niche picked out and a content strategy ready to deploy, it's time to set up a noteworthy account.

How to set up your Instagram

Instagram is mobile only, so you've got my permission at this point to get out your phone while reading this to follow along. Your phone needs to be Apple iOS, Android, Windows 8 or later. As long as it's not an old Nokia or

Motorola (do they still make those?), you'll be good to go.

Head over to the App store (specific to your phone type) and search for Instagram App. It's a free download that should begin instantly. Once you have it installed, it's time to sign up.

Sign up

Use a relevant business email that matches all your other social media profiles if possible. That way you'll have all notifications in one place. It's also important to keep your usernames and brand name as uniform as you can across all platforms. So the Facebook account you just created should match or be very similar to this Instagram page and any other social profile you create.

Your biography

This is where you set up your profile picture. Make sure it's recognizable, crisp, clear and free from clutter. You can decide whether to use a logo instead, but just I recommended on your Facebook Fan page, using your image is better for building an influencer brand. In fact, if you can use the same image across all social platforms, it will be even better.

The recommended profile picture size is a square image of 110 pixels wide by 110 pixels tall.

Next, you have limited characters to share a little about yourself, what you do and your brand. You can add your tagline or brand slogan here, and with a bit of creativity, you can do both if a few sentences. Check out other influencers in your niche market for some inspiration.

The other important thing to add on your bio is a link, which can be added from the "Settings" tab. You only get one link across the whole platform so choose wisely. Of course, you can change it as often as you like but always make sure this link drives traffic to an important landing page or website at all times.

Turn it into a business account

By default, you begin with a personal profile. To use Instagram for business, you have to connect your account to a Facebook Business Page (the one you just created above). Inside your Facebook Page settings on the left side, you should see the Instagram icon at the bottom. Click on it, and you'll be prompted to connect the two accounts and even switch from a personal to a business account. Just follow the instructions, click confirm, and you're all set. Now you can be able to view more detailed insights and analytics of your audience behavior and content performance.

Publish visually appealing content

It's time to start adding images and videos to your Instagram gallery. But in Instagram aesthetics are everything! You cannot be an Instagram influencer without a carefully crafted visually attractive theme. Your photos in the feed should good and represent your brand accurately from the color palette, font, photo arrangement, etc.

Many Instagram influencers identify and follow a specific style of editing their photos to ensure the color is uniform. Tools like VSCO or Lightroom can be a great asset to help you edit your photos. I also know influencers who create epic content using the in-built filters in Instagram so don't feel like you have to make things so complicated but do make sure you don't compromise on quality.

Once you know how to use Instagram for business, you can create Instagram stories to drive engagement and expand your reach.

What are Instagram stories?

These are short videos or photo collections that disappear after 24 hours. At the time of writing this, they are probably the biggest trend on

Instagram with more than 200million Instagram users using Instagram stories daily. It's an effective way to share entertaining heartwarming moments with your followers. You can also get the attention of people who aren't following by adding relevant hashtags or locations.

Most popular niches on Instagram:

If you're wondering whether your niche market would work well on this platform, here is a small list of some of the best performing niches.

- Fitness
- Luxury/ Lifestyle
- Animals
- Travel

- Fashion

- Beauty and Makeup

- Business/entrepreneurship

- Relationships

- Design

- Making money online

- Art

Best practices for growing your Instagram following:

1. Choose hashtags that will enable your content to be found by other Instagram users. When choosing your hashtags, don't always strive for volume. Just because a lot of people visit a specific hashtag doesn't mean they are ideal for your tribe. You want to aim as close as possible to your ideal audience.

2. Post consistently. Most influencers post daily and some even multiple times a day. You must create a schedule for yourself that allows you to regularly put out fresh content so that your audience can get accustomed to receiving communication from you. Studies done reveal that an increase in posting frequency can boost engagement rates. This doesn't mean creating unrealistic schedules for yourself. Be mindful of how you plan out your time, and if you need some help, you can always use tools like Buffer to help you create and publish content in advance.

3. The best times to post on Instagram across industries are 1:00 PM and 5:00 PM, i.e., during lunch break and at the end of the typical workday. The best day to post on Instagram is Friday.

4. Make sure the size of your Instagram images is 1080 pixels wide by 1080 pixels tall. Your Instagram stories should be 1080 pixels wide by 1920 pixels tall, and the maximum file size is 4GB.

5. To succeed in this social platform as an influencer, build a brand that's centered on selling a lifestyle rather than a product. Be inspirational, motivational and inclusive with your copy and speak to both your paying and non-paying clients. If you can find a way to provide your very own splash of unique energy and charisma and create a vivid feed, it will go a long way in establishing what your brand stands for and who it caters to.

6. Cross-promote your dedicated hashtag to all your other profiles. You can also print it in

your print ads, receipts, and other offline activities.

7. Be more active locally. See what's going on in your local neighborhood or a city you're targeting. You can do this by going on the search page and choosing the "Places Tab," then type in the name of the place to see all geotagged posts for that location.

8. Block out some time daily to go through accounts in your niche and "like and comment" other people's photos. You can find relevant users by going through the hashtags you usually use or view the followers of your favorite Instagrammers. Start with 5-10 photos on each person's account to get their attention. Make sure you leave a genuine comment and give them a follow if they resonate.

9. Geotag your photos so that other people who used the same geotag can see your picture and potentially follow you since you now have so much in common.

10. Approach popular users and ask for collaboration. This requires some creative thinking and a generous heart. For example, ask another Instagrammer in your niche if you can "take over their account" for the day as a guest contributor. Instagram story takeovers are a great way to grow your following dramatically, and they can be loads of fun. Test them out!

11. Encourage more User-Generated Content (UGC). By encouraging your growing audience to participate in your journey either through contests, giveaways, etc., and offering

something they would want, your audience is more likely to share pictures of themselves with your product. With a little creativity, you can come up with a great giveaway that doesn't cost you much but generates lots of engagement, sharing, tagging and promotion of your brand organically.

Twitter

Twitter has 313 million monthly active users. It's most known as the go-to platform for customers to discuss brands. This makes it very appealing for a social media influencer who wants to attract an audience of buying customers.

To be an important influencer on this platform, you need to understand the dynamics of Twitter conversations and what your role should be as an influencer.

The most powerful type of Twitter influencer you can become is known as a hub influencer. According to an in-depth study of Twitter conversations done by the Pew Research Group and the Social Media Research

Foundation hub influencers are the key people at the center of their conversational networks. These are the people creating virality by starting movements, creating hashtags and population the trending board. A hub is usually an influential individual or a media organization.

As the center of a conversational network your role as a hub influencer would be to tweet new information to a vast network of followers, then those followers retweet that information.

Becoming a hub as an individual isn't easy. You must consistently produce original information that is noteworthy enough to warrant retweets. You also need to have enough of the right kind of followers to gain retweets.

This takes us back to all the exercises we've done in section one and two of this book. Helping to prepare you, honing down your niche and understand how to attract your ideal audience. Without a definite niche and a tribe, your content (regardless of how fantastic it is) would go nowhere.

Another type of influencer you could become on Twitter is known as a bridge influencer. The difference between being a hub and a bridge influencer is that as a hub influencer you create viral movements and hashtags whereas as a bridge influencer you connect related groups and create virality by sharing relatable content from one group to another. In other words, as a bridge influencer, you don't have to produce information because your primary role is to publicize it. Your influence comes from your positioning. You connect the thoughts and ideas of one group to another and identify relevant points among groups to serve as a channel for that information.

The best and quickest way to become a bridge influencer is to connect with the "hubs" in your niche as well as in niches that have an effect on your primary niche. One of the critical aspects of succeeding as a bridge influencer is being able to understand the conversational structure in which you exist. What do I mean by this?

For example, if you're in a Polarized Crowed (Pew research study defines it as two large dense groups of people that talk about the same subject but do not connect to each other or use the same words), then realize these people don't really interact with other groups. As such you can serve as a link between the polarized network and outside conversations. As you can see, a lot of strategy goes into becoming a Twitter influencer. It has to be very intentional and well planned if you want this to work but once you position yourself either as a hub or bridge you're far more likely to become recognized as a Twitter influencer and consequently reap the rewards.

Before sharing some best practices for both types of Twitter influencers, let's talk about the setup process.

How to set up your Twitter account:

Step one. Your profile name

Head over to the Twitter website and click sign up. One of the first things you'll have to decide is your profile name. This becomes the name or twitter handle you'll have also known as @name.

I recommend using your real name or the name you're using to establish your brand. If you can use the same name as your Facebook Fan page, Instagram account, and Twitter, you create a congruency that helps build your credibility. You'll also want to make the account user your full name as well, and please keep your @name short and memorable otherwise no one will remember it.

Step two. Add a photo of yourself

Please avoid using a logo as much as people. You are a social media influencer. Your personality and relatability will help build up your brand quicker, which means the more people see your face, the better. This image is displayed any time you post a tweet, so you want to differentiate yourself from everyone else in the Twitter ocean. And if you use the same image on Instagram and Facebook, it becomes easier for your followers to spot you on this platform as well. The best recommendation for image size is 400 pixels wide by 400 pixels tall even though it only displays 200 x 200.

Step three. Your twitter bio

Just as with Instagram, you have a limited character bio (160 characters). This is your chance to tell everyone what you do, why you do it and what you're passionate about. Make it exciting and friendly so people can feel comfortable making a connection with you. There are many times I've read a bio and decided to follow that person purely because of how they expressed who they are and what they stand for.

Step four. Add your website or a landing page

Twitter gives you a little section to add your website, any social platform you choose or another landing page. Even if you don't yet have a site utilize this spot to drive people to your Instagram account, Facebook Group or Fan page. If you have a blog or an "about me" page, this is also a great link to use.

Step five. Add a header background Image

A lot of people forget to do this, but as an influencer, that background image is super important. It's your chance to engage your audience and make them curious about you using something visual. This is often the first thing your visitors will see so make it captivating.

The best recommendation for image size is 1,500 pixels wide by 500 pixels tall.

Step six. Follow relevant people

Look at people in your industry that interest you, other influencers that you want to start connecting with and hubs that you want to start learning from. Don't just follow celebrities.

Now that you've followed a few people, it's time to publish your first tweet. The only way to learn and get good at tweeting is to test and experiment. At first, it will seem like you're just talking to the wind, but if you keep at it and build connections with the right people; you'll soon be part of conversations that can build your following. Don't forget to keep an eye on who is talking to you and about you. By regularly checking your "mentions" you'll be able to speak to the right people, respond to those reaching out and establishing yourself as relatable.

Most popular niches on Twitter:

If you're wondering whether your niche market would work well on this platform, here is a small list of some of the best performing niches.

- Celebrity News
- Gaming
- World News
- Sports
- Health and Wellness
- Tech
- Politics
- Travel
- Personal Development
- Digital Marketing

Best practices for growing your Twitter following:

1. Get very niched right from the start and discern the type of information you want to either create or share that will best serve your niche.

2. Do your best to remain relevant and on topic especially on this platform because it's such a fast-paced platform that makes it super easy to be ignored.

3. When starting out on Twitter (especially if you choose to be a hub influencer), you should follow the most significant people in your network. In fact, I recommend connecting to "bridge influencers" so you can quickly become familiar with the subtle nuances of

your niche, the best hashtags, vocabulary to use, etc.

4. Work on building bonds and connections within your chosen niche. These connections are the ones that will help you build momentum and an engaged audience.

5. Be super responsive on Twitter. You must thank those you retweet and reply to your tweets. And please avoid twitter wars at all costs as it only messes with your credibility. Twitter is mainly about making connections and building dialogue so if you want to succeed on the platform align with the nature of the game.

6. The best time to tweet on average is around 8:00 AM - 10:00 AM as well as 6:00 PM - 9:00

PM. If you are in the B2C space, then you can the recommendation is that you post more on weekends while if you are targeting a B2B audience, then weekday tweets will probably work best for you. If you also want to maximize retweets and clickthroughs then aim for noon or 5:00 PM - 6:00 PM.

YouTube

As with every other channel we've talked about so far, this powerful channel (although harder to conquer nowadays) can serve your mission of becoming a highly paid influencer as long as you understand who your audience is and what they want. Video content is perhaps the fastest way to grow your brand and get the attention of your tribe as well as other brands.

YouTube is the second most visited website in existence according to Alexa.

On average, people spend eight minutes and forty-one seconds each day on YouTube. 1.9 billion logged-in users are visiting YouTube every month in 2019. That's literally half the Internet.

Cisco predicts that video will be 82% of all Internet traffic by 2022.

96% of 18 - 24-year-old American Internet users use YouTube, and 85% of 45 - 54-year-olds are using YouTube so if you're worried about reaching your target age group, trust me, everyone can be reached. YouTube has better numbers when it comes to older age groups than Facebook.

The top ten YouTube stars earned 42% more money in 2018 than in previous years meaning; the demand for influencers continues to grow. Forbes estimates that these ten men earned a combined total of $180.5 million in 2018. There's no denying the potential for non-traditional marketing with macro or micro-influencers is expanding, and it's not too late for you to grab your piece of the pie.

How to set up your YouTube Channel:

Step One. To set up a YouTube channel, you need a Google account

So first, head over to Google and create your account if you haven't done so already. Once you have the account, you can easily find the YouTube icon by clicking on the navigation menu on the right corner of your Gmail.

Step Two. Sign in to YouTube and click on the user icon at the top right of the screen

You should be able to see a gear icon that will lead you into your account's "YouTube Settings." Click on "Create a new Channel," decide on the name (again I recommend following the same as the other social platforms to create brand congruency). Add your brand name and click create.

Step Three. Fill in the "About" section

This is where you will fill out your profile and channel description. Here you should describe your brand and what viewers can expect to see on your channel. This is also where you can add links to the other social media networks as well as your website. Please keep in mind that this description will appear in more than one place on your channel so be thoughtful, implement some of the copy that you came up with for your brand messaging and elevator pitch.

Step Four. Upload a cover photo for your channel

The first thing visitors see when they come to your YouTube channel is the cover photo so use this to introduce people to your brand. Give them a visual experience of what you have to offer as a brand and a person. The more aligned this cover photo is with your brand style, messaging as well as the other cover photos used on Twitter, Facebook and other social networks the more enhanced their perception will be about you.

The recommended dimension for your cover photo is 2560 pixels wide by 1440 pixels tall with a maximum file size of 4MB.

Step Five. Publish your video content

It's time to start making some magic with your video content. Assuming you have implemented everything we discussed earlier in the book, you are now fully equipped to produce world-class content. And no, you don't need fancy equipment or a big production team to publish videos that your audience will love. If you own a smartphone and an earpiece you are ready to produce amazing videos. As long as you know who you're targeting and what message you want to share, hit the record button, speak to the camera, edit it, upload it and publish.

Test out different types of videos relevant to the niche market you are serving and be sure to add in lots of inspirational content as well.

Having variety in your video content is a great way to start testing what resonates most with your growing audience.

Step Six. Optimize for video search and Google search

Your video ranks on Google as well as YouTube search, did you know that?

To make sure it's optimized for ranking fill in the title, description and tags sections when uploading a video. These are essential if you want your video to be easily discoverable so don't overlook this part. Have a keyword strategy in place and optimize every video for the Keywords you want to rank for. Given the fact that YouTube is a Google-owned product, by implementing some SEO on your videos you'll find yourself ranking on both search engines.

Step Seven. Create a channel Trailer

Create an amazing introduction using a channel trailer and make sure you grab the attention of your new visitor within the first 5 - 10 seconds.

This trailer is usually a short and sweet video that introduces your new visitor to your channel. It's a great way to welcome the visitor and let him or her know who you are, what your brand is all about and what kind of content they can expect to see in the future.

Step Eight. Integrate your channel with your website and social media networks

If you have a website, you can add a YouTube widget to help drive website visitors to your channel. YouTube also allows you to connect your associated site to your channel which helps a lot with search results and also as a form of verification that your website is the official brand owner of the channel.

You can also start sharing the content you create to all your other social platforms. A good trick that I like to use is creating shorter "teaser videos" for my Instagram and encouraging people to go watch the full video on YouTube. It seems to work very well on Instagram and is worth testing on Twitter as well.

Step Nine. Engage with your growing audience

As with all social platforms, interaction and engagement is everything. You must build a community around your channel. Reply to comments, ask and answer questions and more importantly, listen to your people and what they have to say. Your viewers watch your content and share their insights because they are interested in you. Give them more of what they want, and you'll have a very active community. Gary Vaynerchuck is an excellent example of how powerful YouTube can be if you are continually creating interactive and engaging content.

Most popular niches on YouTube:

If you're wondering whether your niche market would work well on this platform, here is a small list of some of the best performing niches.

- Tech Videos.

- Gaming

- Food

- Fashion

- Beauty

- Travel

- Animals

- Comedy/ Humor

- Product Reviews

- How To's

Best practices for growing your YouTube community:

1. Invest enough time coming up with creative and engaging intros for your videos. You only have less than ten seconds to grab someone's attention and get him or her hooked to your channel so make it count right from the get-go.

2. Develop emotional sharpness and find fresh ways of expressing this in your videos. Your video has to be moving. It has to make you laugh, cry, ponder profound questions, learn something you didn't know, think in a certain way and engage your curiosity. It should also be sharp enough to evoke a specific reaction from your audience. They should either decide to love your work or hate it. You don't want to be an in-betweener! This is where we get back

to the earlier exercises we did in this book where we determined how we want your audience to feel when interacting with your content. Focus on how you want them to feel rather than executing a perfect script.

3. Be different in your niche. Use your brand to express your own unique voice. If you do your research well, you'll be able to know what's missing in your niche and what other influencers in your niche are doing that's working, and also that's not working. By knowing what "the crowd" is doing, you now have a springboard from which to create your unique concept offering something fresh that does ultimately help you stand out. All this is possible if you do your research well.

4. Use branded thumbnails in your videos. Make sure your YouTube channel stands out and becomes easily recognizable by adding some cool customized thumbnails to your videos.

5. Always have a visible "Subscribe" call to action in every published video. You can use annotations where relevant or just add something that aligns with your branding style as you're editing the video so that it blends in seamlessly with your content.

6. Promote your videos on your other social platforms. Share your videos on Facebook, Twitter, LinkedIn, Pinterest, Scoop.it, and any other relevant platform.

7. Shoot in HD or higher quality and make sure the audio quality is excellent. Nothing will turn off your audience faster than a video that of poor quality and poor audio. This is super important, so please invest in the right equipment.

8. Use YouTube cards to reduce abandonment and boost engagement. The longer someone stays on your channel, the longer they are active on YouTube (so YouTube rewards users who can hold the attention of the audience). Using your video analytics, you can be able to see the exact point people tend to lose interest and abandon your video, and then you can place YouTube cards at that point to hold their attention and potentially get them to click on other videos.

9. Add a sub confirmation to all your YouTube links. This is a low hanging fruit that many influencers fail to utilize. You can implement on your other social media channels as well as your website. All you need to do is to use the sub_confirmation link when sharing the link to your YouTube channel (instead of just using the regular link). When a user clicks on this sub_confirmation link, the first thing they'll see on the YouTube is a popup asking them to subscribe to your channel. Go ahead, add it on now and watch as more subscribers start showing up as you go about sharing your videos.

Chapter 08: Taking your brand from unknown to influential

Going from zero influence on social media to building a personal brand that's well known with thousands (even millions) of followers is not that complicated. Anyone can do it, but few do because the hard part is the daily grind that goes into building up the momentum. Overnight success is real. It just takes years of preparation and momentum building before that tipping point occurs. To be fair, not all influencers are overnight successes.

Take for example two YouTubers in different niche markets. One girl (a videographer) went from 3,000 subscribers to 150,000 subscribers within a two-week time frame. The reason for this "overnight success" was the fact that she had been creating fantastic content for more than 2 years and built an active community around her brand. And at some point, she decided to create an exclusive video for a famous artist that she admired and asked her community members to share and circulate the video and tag the artist so that he could see this video inspired by him. Her community shared it all across Twitter, and the buzz created a big enough wave to get his attention, which led to him retweeting and commenting. Of course, the YouTuber's reach expanded and within two weeks she exponentially exploded her growth and got a chance to communicate and offer her services to the artist. Overnight success? Of course. But it was two years in the making!

There's another girl I want to tell you about. She's the YouTuber building a brand in the beauty and makeup niche. Her current following is at 450,000 subscribers and she's made it all from scratch since she was in high school. She now does campaigns with brands like Avon and for a young girl barely in her mid-twenties, she's earning an excellent income. Her success did not experience any sudden spikes. She slowly built the brand one subscriber at a time over the years. It was her patience, passion for her topic and amazing content that has continued to build momentum to the point where brands were willing to give her pitch a try.

So you see dear influencer, the road to your fame and riches is not set in stone. There is also no shortcut to it. The time it takes to become famous is unknown but what is certain is that if you stay on your path and do the work without compromise or loss of enthusiasm, discipline, and passion, you will win.

To go from known to influential, you must be consistent. And I don't just mean publishing your content once a week, I suggest doing it for years. The people that end up creating influential brands are those that stick with it long term. You also need to experiment with various media types. That means podcasting, video, blogging, etc. Your tribe will most likely have different desires on the type of content they want to consume. The more you can satiate their different preferences by appealing to their tastes, the more you'll draw them in. This doesn't mean you need to produce different content for video, podcasting and written material. It means you need to get creative and include a repurposing plan within your current content strategy.

Another essential fact to reiterate here is that you must genuinely care about your audience. Again this goes back to the exercises we did in section one of this book. If you don't know why you're doing this and if you don't really feel that people should believe in you and have confidence in your ideas because you genuinely care about serving them in a certain way, then it's going to be tough becoming a social media influencer.

Social media is about socializing and exchanging ideas. It's about caring for each other and listening to each other. You need to become that person that helps others out, the reliable, caring, trustworthy virtual friend. That's not something you can fake. So if you genuinely do care about your people and feel you are the right person for your topic then keep forging your path because you are bound to receive the great harvest of online influence.

With that influence comes the added benefit of having brands write you a check just for being you and doing your thing. Not too bad right?

Well, before you get all excited about that check, it's important I mention that it won't just fall out of the sky. If you really want to earn some good money, there are some things you need to get right. Let's address that next.

The pitch the pricing structure and charging what you're worth

If you are serious about becoming a social media influencer by any means, then I certainly recommend taking the time to work on your mindset as well as the pitch you make to companies, sponsors, editors and more. I have learned over the years that there are definite ways you can help your prospects receive communications from you with an open mind.

Due to the novelty of our industry, brands, and business owners are still very skeptical about dealing with influencers or getting into influencer marketing because they worry about getting ripped off, shafted or slandered online. They also struggle with understanding how to measure the ROI of their investments. Knowing this, I am dedicating some space to share tips about how you can craft the perfect pitch once you are ready to take the plunge.

Before sharing the tips, however, I need to call out the elephant in the room. Why? Because it's perhaps the biggest obstacle to an influencer's financial success. You can be great at nurturing a community and building a brand, but if you have mindset blocks around selling, you'll continue to be broke. It will be hard to close deals with other companies and making an offer to your audience will feel incongruent and ultimately lead to little action from your wide audience. To help you with that, you need to work on your current mindset around money and selling.

You must charge what you are worth, not too much and indeed not too little. Since it's still pretty much the wild wild west when it comes to pricing for influencer marketing, I encourage you to find price points for your services that enable you to deliver excellent value for excellent pay. And reiterating what I said before if the mindset is an issue, you better work on those money blocks!

Now, let's talk about how to craft the perfect pitch:

Tip One. Use a warm, friendly but professional tone

Your tone really matters when giving a pitch. In influencer marketing, it's not about being overly formal and pretentious. Be yourself, use the same tone that you portray on your brand so that as businesses check out your work, it will feel congruent. It is possible to be casual friendly and professional at the same time. I find this works best.

Tip Two. Find a specific contact and name

Unless it's just utterly impossible to send a personalized email to a specific contact, I recommend doing your research and getting hold of one particular person. This tactic usually warrants a quicker response.

Tip Three. Gain insights on your audience demographics

Getting to know who is in your tribe is super important. You might discover there is a slight variation in demographics as you move from one platform to another. Having this information will help you know how to serve best your community, which brands to work with and what products/services will be more appealing to the various platforms you dominate.

This is the first crucial step before pitching any brand because as a general rule, your audience will want to know things like where your audience lives, average age group, gender, etc. The valuable insights you offer to a brand during the pitch process, the more you can negotiate and demonstrate expertise.

Tip Four. Make sure you do your homework on the brand

Never approach a brand unless you feel confident you already understand enough about their marketing, how they like to communicate with their target audience and the value you see yourself bringing to the table that further enhances whatever they are currently doing. Think of this pitch from their point of view; not yours.

Ideally, you want to be able to show businesses that by working with you they will reach their objective or even surpass it. Some research questions to get your juices flowing are - What channels are they active across? Are you already doing any influencer marketing campaigns? Who is their target market? What products are you interested in promoting the most?

Tip Five. Explain what you do in no more than 2 sentences and describe yourself in 5 words or less

Yes, you read me right! You need to keep that intro as short and sharp as possible. Don't write too much when approaching a cold lead. People are so busy nowadays and have very low attention spans so if you don't keep the entire pitch brief, and to the point, you'll probably lose their interest and never get a response.

When describing yourself, use a distinctive title or phrase that will cause the reader to think, "hmm, that sounds interesting" or "I'd like to hear more." When explaining what you offer always make the brand feel that your offer is equivalent or higher in value than what you're asking for. This is called the 51/49 strategy, i.e., give more than expected.

An example template:

Hey [insert name]

I hope your week is off to a great start! My name is Kendra, I'm an influencer, and I write the Canadian-based blog, [insert website], you can see some of my recent posts here. In the last year, I've grown my IG following to over 19k highly engaged followers. I'm reaching out because I'm currently in planning mode for the

3rd quarter in which I'll be working on quite a few fitness posts. In particular, I've been dying to try out [X fitness brand] high-performance compression tights and would be interested in doing a review on my site (typically valued at $300). My 12,000 weekly readers have been asking for a Q&A post on fitness products so I thought this would make for a great organic partnership! Is that something you'd be open to? Please let me know your thoughts - would love to team up on this!

Side note. I consider a rejection a response too. By receiving an answer back (whether it's an answer you like or not), gives you an opportunity to learn, get feedback and see where to improve.

Tip Six. Know your worth

As I mentioned before, you need to be able to charge what you're worth. If you don't know your value, even your pitch won't come across strong and genuine enough. Earning money as an influencer means you must be good at influencing - both paying and non-paying clients.

The more data and insights you have about your community engagement, who they are and how responsive they are to you, the easier it will be to pitch with confidence because you'll have proof of the monetary value you want in exchange for your efforts. Show the brands specifics about your "influence" to help the brand increase their confidence in you and then, price yourself accordingly.

In summary, the critical aspects to a great pitch once you've done your homework and feel ready to start pitching small and large companies is to:

1. Describe and show the brand why you are the best micro or macro influencer to work with.

2. Talk about your fantastic audience and let them know specifics about demographics etc.

3. Lay out your offer and detail why it would make sense from their point of view as a brand to invest in your fees.

4. Use evidence to back up your offer. Include your stats, case studies, analytics, and more data!

Chapter 09: The Eleven step formula if you're just getting started

Always think big and start small. Baby steps taken sequentially and consistently will ultimately take you to the top of the mountain.

Step 1: Do a self-audit and get your mindset right.

Have a point of view. Know yourself really well. Why should your tribe listen to you? Why should people follow you? Figure out who you are at the deepest core and what your mission is. What's your polarizing point of view that will definitely not please everybody but will totally attract the right people to you?

Step 2: Pick a niche.

Today you might have one or zero followers; one day you may have 200,000 followers. How you get there fast is by starting out as the expert among your friends and peers. Then work toward being the expert in your city and state. Lastly, launch your global empire. It starts with just one vertical, following that thread into mastery and then expanding from there. This is what a niche will enable you to accomplish, and that's why you need to complete all the practical exercises in section one and two to hone down what your niche will be, what your passionate about and what your brand style will be to embody and compliment that chosen subject matter.

Step 3: Identify and define your ideal audience.

Take the time to hone down your ideal audience so you can build a tribe that positions you as a person of influence. The best way to do this is by getting into the mind of your ideal audience. You must do empathy mapping and really understand who they are, what they care about, where they are hanging out online and what motivates them.

Equipped with this knowledge you can now create content and a brand that is worthy of being followed. People today want to find meaning in the brands they follow. It's your job to show them why they should be supporting and having faith in your ideas.

Step 4: Create a content strategy and marketing plan

Once you have a niche and know the tribe you're marketing to, it's time to build out your strategy. Dive deep into the marketing and content strategy outline provided in this book. Be sure to experiment with a variety of media content, plan for repurposing strategies and any advertising if applicable to you.

Step 5: Select your channels

Whichever platform you choose to start with, learn as much as you can about it. Because each social network hosts varying users, the channel you select will require its own strategy. And when you expand to a new channel, you'll have to create a totally different strategy. Take the information shared in section four and let it guide your approach to growing organically the type of audience you wish to serve.

Step 6: Network within the Industry

To be influential, you need to make real connections both online and offline. Sitting at home on your couch will not get you results. Get out in the world and attend major events related to your niche. Venture outside of social media and participate in real life conversations and gatherings so you can enhance your reputation, influence, and connections.

Step 7: Engage with your community

I encourage you to be very proactive when it comes to responding to your tribe. But don't stop there. Start conversations, ask questions, create debates, etc. The more you can engage with the community the further you will spread your influence. This includes even outside your own feed. Post in groups, tag other influencers and respond to interesting conversations that other influencers have started.

Step 8: Consistently publish fresh world-class content

After devoting an entire chapter on content creation, suffice it to say the quality of content you produce will determine your quality of success as a creative influencer on social media. This will be the foundation that elevates or destroys your brand perception so make sure you give it everything you've got.

Step 9: Quantify your efforts with data

Make sure you're tracking, measuring and collecting all your data as you grow. Each social site shows you insights that help you understand your audience better, the performance of your content as well as paid ads campaigns. Use this to your advantage. Keep a record of everything especially as you start growing because these stats, analytics, case studies and other types of data will become invaluable when you're ready to pitch to companies looking to get into influencer marketing.

Step 10: Collaborate and reach out to influencers in your space

To quickly become an influencer, you'll need to know and hang out with a few influencers yourself. Who you are following is almost as important as who follows you. Reaching out to other influencers is an excellent way for you to get exposure and share your message in the marketplace in ways you otherwise wouldn't be able to on your own. Just make sure you do this from a place of "giving" rather than "getting."

Step 11: Reach out to paying brands and start monetizing your brand

At this point, you started from scratch with nothing, and you now have influencer friends, a growing tribe of loyal fans and data that can help you back up your influencer pitch to paying brands. It's not time to advocate for your brand and reach out to the right companies that are either already doing influencer marketing or want to do influencer marketing.

Never sit and wait for an opportunity to come knocking. If you feel it's time to start promoting and monetizing your brand, then it is time. Grab your tools and media kit, compose that perfect pitch and start teaming up with brands that are dying to see better results with their marketing. Don't forget to use the customizable template that I shared with you when you start reaching out to companies. And by all means, shoot for the stars!

The next step on your influencer journey

Now that you have found your unique identity on social media and you know how to set yourself up for success as an influencer, it's time to start implementing the plan. Be consistent, stick to your strategy until you gain some traction. You've now found your little corner on social media to grow yourself and build a brand an audience that helps you live out your mission.

Persist on this path of becoming an authority figure in your niche and master just one platform at a time (whether that'll be Facebook, YouTube or Instagram first), to massively improve your chances of exponential success. Focus on depth and concentrate your energy on one vertical rather than trying to be everywhere all at once. This is how you'll take your business to the next level where scaling up becomes the natural consequence.

By implementing everything, I've outlined in this book, you will naturally stand out from the crowd and sooner rather than later, other brands will start to notice you. That's when the money will start pouring in. But you can't keep your eyes on the money; stay focused on doing your thing and serving your tribe. Each and every platform discussed has the potential to make you very wealthy as an influencer, and I assume by now, you have at least set up your accounts following the step-by-step guidance I gave you. Within your grasp is the chance to become an influencer and change lives (including your own), but you must be willing to put in the work.

Overnight success doesn't come to those who just sit and wait. You might have no followers at the moment, but as you keep adding value to the marketplace and mastering your craft, you'll start growing your followers faster than you could have imagined. This is a world that rewards action so whatever you do next, make sure it is activity geared toward the realization of your dreams. And lastly, remember, no one really cares unless you can help with something they care about. Now go out there and gain some influence!

Recommended Resources:

Want to learn even more about taking your already established brand to the next level? Here are some additional resources that I have found useful.

Influencer: Building your personal brand in the age of social media - https://www.amazon.com/Influencer-Building-Personal-Brand-Social/dp/0806538856

The rise of social influencers: A new age of digital marketing - http://blog.influence.co/rise-of-social-influencers/